GREEN &BLACK'S

ORGANIC

ULTIMATE

CHOCOLATE RECIPES
THE NEW COLLECTION

GREEN & BLACK'S
ORGANIC

ULTIMATE

Chocolate Recipes
The New Collection

PHOTOGRAPHY
BY JENNY ZARINS

EDITED BY MICAH CARR-HILL

KYLE BOOKS

Micah's Acknowledgements

This book would not have been possible without Anita who championed it from the start and has worked tirelessly, ensuring it came to fruition. Thanks babe.

I'd like to thank Kyle and Sophie; Kyle for originally suggesting a second book, and convincing us that there was room for another book of chocolate recipes from Green & Black's, and Sophie for putting up with my endless excuses of why I hadn't typed up or checked another recipe.

As editor of this book I've had, some think, the enviable task of tasting all the recipes we tested, a lot of which never made it but still had to be cooked and tasted, sometimes two or three times. Thanks to Georgie and Sylvain for recipe testing (I did do my own though, honest) and putting up with my often damning comments about something they'd just spent a good while slaving over.

Thanks to Jenny for taking such beautiful photographs, especially those of my daughter, Gabriella, who took the time out of her busy schedule to show me how baking should actually be done.

Thank you, Jo, for asking all your celebrity friends for their favourite chocolate recipes. They have certainly done justice to your (and Craig's) original creation all those years ago: Green & Black's 70% dark chocolate.

To all those who contributed a recipe to the book, I thank you.

And finally, thanks to my family; the aforementioned baking genius, Gabriella, my little man, Noah, and my gorgeous wife, Natalie, who put up with my grumbles after having to taste another boring cake (there are lots out there, I assure you, but not in this book) and my grumpy mornings after cooking into the early hours once they had gone to bed.

Published in 2010 by Kyle Books,
an imprint of Kyle Cathie Ltd. www.kylecathie.com

Distributed by
National Book Network,
4501 Forbes Blvd., Suite 200, Lanham, MD 20706
Phone: (800) 462-6420 Fax: (301) 429-5746
custserv@nbnbooks.com

10 9 8 7 6 5 4 3 2 1

ISBN 978-1-906868-32-1
Library of Congress Control No. 2010934445

Text copyright © 2010 by Cadbury Holdings Limited*
Photographs copyright © 2010 by Jenny Zarins
Design copyright © 2010 by Kyle Cathie Limited

Design: heredesign.co.uk
Photography: Jenny Zarins
Project editor: Sophie Allen
Food stylist: Lizzie Harris
Props stylist: Tabitha Hawkins
Recipe testing: Georgina Fuggle & Sylvain Jamois
Copy editor: Stephanie Evans
Production: Gemma John

Color reproduction by Sang Choy
Printed and bound in Italy by Printer Trento

*Except for all recipes acknowledged on pages 6-7

Mixed Sources
Product group from well-managed forests and other controlled sources
www.fsc.org Cert no. CQ-COC-000012
© 1996 Forest Stewardship Council

FSC

CONTENTS

ACKNOWLEDGMENTS

We would like to thank the following chefs, authors, publishers and fans of the brand for giving us permission to use their recipes:

Tom Aikens, Chocolate Tart (p81), Chocolate Crêpes (p200) *tomaikens.co.uk*

Donna Air, Chocolate-drizzled Fruity Oat Bars (p28) *donnaair.com*

Omar Allibhoy, Churros and Chocolate a la Española (p183) *elpiratadetapas.co.uk*

Darina Allen, Chocolate and Peanut Butter Pie (p88), from *Easy Entertaining* (Kyle Cathie 2005), Gluten-free Chocolate Fudge Pudding (p97), from *Healthy Gluten-free Eating* (Kyle Cathie, 2004) *cookingisfun.ie*

L'Artisan du Chocolat, Chocolate Martini (p204), Matcha (Green Tea)White Chocolate New Orleans Fizz (p205) *artisanduchocolat.com*

Lindsey Bareham, Chocolate, Almond, and Raspberry Birthday Cake (p66), Chocolate and Chestnut Soufflé Cake (p70), *lindseybareham.com*

Annie Bell, Guilt-free Chocolate Cake (p58), Bûche de Noël (p116) from *Gorgeous Cakes* (Kyle Cathie 2005)

Richard Bertinet, Dark Chocolate and Cardamom Ice Cream (p164), *thebertinetkitchen.com*

Charmaine Bustard, Farmhouse Chocolate Banana Bread (p54)

Adam Byatt, Ultimate Chocolate Soufflé (p154) *trinityrestaurant.co.uk*

Millie Charters, Chocolate Pudding Pie (p90)

Sally Clarke, Bitter Chocolate and Buttermilk Ice Cream (p160) *sallyclarke.com*

Harry Eastwood, Heartache Chocolate Cake (p63), from *Red Velvet & Chocolate Heartache* (Bantam Press, 2009) *harryeastwood.com*

Maria Elia, Retro Cherry Chocolate and Almond Jelly Roll (p106) *thisismariaelia.com*

The English Cheesecake Company, Choctastic Cheesecake (p148) *englishcheesecake.com*

Kellie Fernandes, Chocolate Chip Cookies (p16)

Jane Ford, Jane's Chocolate Christmas Pudding (p114)

Georgina Fuggle, Truly Gooey Chocolate and Hazelnut Cookies (p20), White Chocolate and Blackberry Cupcakes (p42), Ginger and Dark Chocolate Roulade with Poached Pears (p108), Pistachio and Fig Chocolate Biscotti (p192) *thehartandfuggle.com*

Paul Gayler, Dark Chocolate, Brandy, and Cherry Cake (p64), White Chocolate and Lemon Cheesecake Ice Cream (p162), Milk Chocolate Rum and Raisin Semi-freddo (p166) *paulgayler.com*

The Ginger Gourmand, Chocolate Panna Cotta with Vanilla Poached Pears (p149) *thegingergourmand.blogspot.com*

Good Housekeeping **magazine,** Chocolate and Pecan Pie (p94), Marbled Mousse (p122), Chocolate Iced Mille Feuilles (p170) *allaboutyou.com/goodhousekeeping*

Guerrilla Gardening, Chocolate Seed Bombs (p188) *GuerrillaGardening.org*

Arianna Halshaw of Bittersweet Bakers, Chocolate Cinnamon Rolls (p51) *bittersweetbakers.com*

Anna Hansen, Chocolate Liquorice Delice with Cocoa Chile Wafer (p129) *themodernpantry.co.uk*

Alice Hart, Velvet Salted Caramel Chocolate

Torte (p78) *thehartandfuggle.com*

Maida Heatter, Brownie Crisps (p18)

Harriet Hewitson, Pear and Chocolate Tatin (p82)

Felicity Hood, Chocolate and Raspberry Cheesecake Brownies (p36)

Simon Hopkinson, Chocolate Pithiviers (p197), from *Roast Chicken and Other Stories* (Ebury Press 1999)

The Hummingbird Bakery, Ginger Chocolate Cupcakes (p44), Dark Chocolate Cupcakes (p45) *hummingbirdbakery.com*

Sam Hutchins, Chocolate Fritters (p190), 32 Great Queen Street, WC2B 5AA

Sylvain Jamois, 5-minute Chocolate Pudding (p124) *undercoverkitchen.com*

Judges Bakery, Chocolate Cupcakes (p38) *judgesbakery.com*

Hanne Kinniburgh, Strawberry and White Chocolate Cheesecake (p146)

Thierry Laborde, White Chocolate and Passion Fruit Delice (p128) *visitthekitchen.com*

Rose Levy Beranbaum, Chocolate Layer Cake (p60) *realbakingwithrose.com*

Prue Leith, Ultimate Chocolate Roulade (p110) *Leiths Cookery Bible* by Prue Leith and Caroline Waldegrave (Bloomsbury Publishing 2003)

Lulu, Mint Chocolate Bombs (p156), *trullorestaurant.com*

Nick Malgieri, Chocolate Bourbon Cake (p77), *nickmalgieri.com*

Marianne Magnier Moreno, Almost Oreos (p22) from *Cooking from Above: Baking* (Hamlyn 2009)

Emma Marijewycz, Chocolate-orange Ginger Biscotti (p194)

Mary McCartney, Chocolate and Coconut Rice Pudding (p132) *marymccartney.com*

Allegra McEvedy, Not Millionaire's Shortbread (p24) *allegramcevedy.com*

Rachael Nimento, Chocolate Tiffin (p27)

Sharon Osbourne, Strawberry Pâte de Fruit (p184) *sharonosbourne.com*

Lorraine Pascale, Chocolate Banoffee Tart (p84) *ellasbakehouse.co.uk*

Antony Perring, Chocolate and Raspberry Croissant Pudding (p100) *antonyperring.com*

José Pizarro, Olive Oil Chocolate Cake (p111) *josepizarro.com*

Primrose Bakery, Peanut Butter Cupcakes (p40) *primrosebakery.org.uk*

Claudia Roden, Gateau au Chocolat (p68), from *The Book of Jewish Food* (Penguin 1999)

Rick Rodgers, Chocolate Ricotta Cheesecake (p144)

Denise Rowe, All-in-one Spiced Chocolate Loaf (p56)

Mark Sargeant, Spiced Chocolate Cream (p136) *theswanwestmalling.co.uk*

Hannah Saxton, Vanilla Cream Truffles (p196) *mychocolate.co.uk*

Natalie Seldon of Estella Cupcakes, Ultimate Chocolate Fudge Cake (p73) *estellacupcakes.com*

James Tanner, Chocolate Fondant (p96), from *James Tanner Takes 5* (Kyle Cathie 2010)

Jo Wood, Thyme and Chocolate Truffles (p202) *jowoodorganics.com*

Charles Worthington, White Chocolate and Cardamom Rice Pudding with Marmalade and Cointreau Sauce (p134) *cwlondon.com*

Paul a. Young, Pure Gold Sea Salted Chocolate Ginger Tart with Fennel Seed Brittle (p86), paul.a.young fine chocolates – *paulayoung.co.uk*

JO FAIRLEY'S FOREWORD

Green & Black's has never just been for eating, square by square. Right from the word "go," we realized that Green & Black's-lovers were making the most of our dark chocolate, in particular, to create a wide range of temptations—mostly cakes, cookies, desserts, but also (occasionally), using it to "turbo-charge" a stew, or give a new dimension to something like coq au vin (for our non-vegetarian fans...)

It seems extraordinary now in these days of widespread chocolate connoisseurship, but when we launched Green & Black's—the world's very first organic chocolate—back in 1991, it was also the very first 70% cocoa solids option on the market in the UK (our home territory). Elsewhere, the virtues of 70% dark chocolate had long been understood. (Not least by slender Frenchwomen who often told

me they kept a bar of Green & Black's in their desk drawer, to have a square at 4 p.m. which would keep them going till dinner...)

What we swiftly saw after we launched Green & Black's was that for everyone from TV chefs to dedicated home cooks via magazines' food editors, 70% chocolate became the benchmark for cooking with. And so it made sense to us, pretty soon, to put together a recipe leaflet, with wonderful recipes like Linda McCartney's brownies and The Groucho Club's gooey chocolate treats. That later grew into the first Green & Black's cookbook, which has won cook-lit prizes and become a bestseller (half a million copies, worldwide, and counting).

By popular request—ta-dah!—this is the second Green & Black's recipe book, showcasing recipes from many of the fans we've picked up along the way—using many of the different flavors we've since launched, as well as the "classic" dark chocolate and our cooking chocolates. We were flattered as anything that when it came to collecting the recipes, virtually everyone we asked said "yes" in less time than it takes to measure out a tablespoon of cocoa powder. (Except Twiggy, who turned us down saying: "I'm not a big dessert cook and the only thing I can think of to do with the wonderful Green & Black's Chocolate is to eat it!") We know the real reason that our "Green & Black's Fan Club" is so extensive is that we make sublime chocolate—still created in an artisan way with enormous attention to detail and perfectionism—but we also know that the extra "feel-good" factor that comes with buying a bar of Green & Black's is important, too.

We've come a long, long way from the bedroom where Green & Black's was born one rainy Saturday night. ("Green" because we were organic, "black" because—with that oh-so-important 70% cocoa— we had the darkest chocolate on the market at the time.) But the reality is that since Green & Black's launch in 1991, we've seen with our own eyes the huge difference that our chocolate has made to the communities that we work with (and are committed to continue to work with). In Belize, where there was no secondary education before we started trading with the Maya, 70% of schoolchildren (and counting) now go on to secondary school—and many are moving into further education. The skills they bring back to their communities will help these farming families travel further along the path out of poverty. And it's with huge pride that Green & Black's made the announcement that by the end of 2011, every single bar of Green & Black's (with all their myriad ingredients) will be carrying the FAIRTRADE Mark.

I once asked Cayetano Ico, the head of the Toledo Cacao Grower's Association in Belize, if he had a message for Green & Black's lovers. "Tell them that when they buy a bar of chocolate, they're sending a child to school," he said. And I can't imagine a nicer thought, as I naughtily dip my finger in swirly dark cake mixture, or serve up a chocolate pudding or a mousse to friends. Or simply break off a square. (If I'm pretending to be a disciplined Frenchwoman.) Or, more likely, two or three or four...

Jo Fairley

Co-founder, Green & Black's

INTRODUCTION

It's been seven years since our Green & Black's first book was published. It was a truly eclectic mix of recipes from sweet to savoury, complex to simple, and soufflés to sausages that were sourced from friends and relatives, people from the world of food, and a smattering of celebrities.

We've decided to theme this book more around baking—with chocolate, of course—as this has been increasingly fashionable over the last few years; a need for culinary comfort one may say. We've gathered our recipes from the same sources—family, friends, chefs, writers, and celebrities—although it has been up to me to come up with a few more than last time.

I'd like to think that this will be a baking book that will be of interest to men as well as women. Despite men's increased interest in food and cooking, baking still has the reputation of something that does not concern men. Nonsense I say. Let's show the female bakers of the world that we can wear an apron with pride and whip up a chocolate sponge cake as well as the next woman.

Being a book largely about baking, chemistry plays a far more important role than in much savory cooking and if we don't use the right proportions of ingredients, the best preparation methods, and the correct temperatures then the results can be disappointing. Baking is not for the casual cook who says, "I never look at cookbooks, I just look in the fridge and throw a few things together." As an aside, I don't trust people who say this unless they are professional cooks. When people ask me why something was over or under cooked that they roasted or baked I reply with the same question: "Do you have an oven thermometer?" Invariably the answer is no. "Go and buy one and use it and then come back to me if you have a problem," I tell them. Invariably I don't see them again, but probably because they think I'm a bit of a jerk.

At Green & Black's we've always sourced the best possible organic ingredients for our chocolate and have worked closely with cocoa farming communities providing us with our cocoa. Our Maya Gold bar was the UK's first Fairtrade certified product. When developing and testing these recipes we used organic and Fairtrade ingredients wherever possible. I would urge you to do the same if and when possible. If we do not respect the ground food is grown in or raised on, and the farmers that go to the effort of growing the best tasting food they can, free from artificial chemicals and pesticides, then who knows what we, and our children, will end up eating in years to come. Lecture over.

Not all these recipes will be new (didn't someone once say that there was no such thing as an original idea; does that apply to recipes as well?) but I hope that you agree that they are amongst the best. When developing new bars of chocolate I am always looking at the familiar (there's a good reason why chocolate is popular and carob isn't: chocolate tastes good) and the nostalgic. Tastes and smells remain in our memory throughout our lives and I love it when a particular food brings memories flooding back of when I was a child and I ate that food for the first time. But first and foremost I'm looking not only to match expectations but exceed them. It is only then that I feel I've done my job properly.

Lastly, I can only hope that this book becomes well stained, mainly with chocolate mind you, as it is only this that will prove it to be a cookbook of worth.

ALL OVENS I'VE EVER USED, CHEAP OR EXPENSIVE, ARE INACCURATELY CALIBRATED.

THIS MEANS THAT WHAT IT SAYS ON THE DIAL OR DIGITAL DISPLAY IS UNTRUSTWORTHY.

BAKING IS MORE CHEMISTRY EXPERIMENT THAN COOKING AND DOESN'T WORK WELL IF THE MEASUREMENTS ARE WRONG (WEIGHTS AND TEMPERATURES).

IF YOU DON'T ALREADY HAVE ONE, BUY AN OVEN THERMOMETER.

THEY COST ABOUT TEN DOLLARS.

AND SOME DECENT SCALES. MY DIGITAL SCALES SET ME BACK A MERE $40.

TEATIME

CHOCOLATE CHIP COOKIES

Makes 16

9 tablespoons unsalted butter
½ cup superfine sugar
¼ cup muscovado sugar
1 large free-range egg
Few drops vanilla extract
1 cup all-purpose flour
½ teaspoon baking
　powder
½ teaspoon salt
¾ cup rolled oats
7oz dark (70% cocoa
　solids) or milk chocolate
　(amount depends on
　your level of addiction),
　chopped into chunks

This is a great recipe for moms, dads, and kids to do together. You can use any flavor of chocolate, just make sure the chunks are a reasonable size. You can make them more "adult" by adding ground ginger.

Preheat the oven to 350°F.

Cream the butter and sugars together in a bowl until smooth. Beat in the egg and vanilla. Add the flour, baking powder, salt, and oats and mix in the chocolate to form a dough. Set aside in the fridge for around 10 minutes to firm up.

Take small balls of dough about the size of a plum and roll them in your hands. Place on a baking sheet lined with parchment paper, spacing them apart to allow for them spreading as they cook. Flatten each ball slightly with your hand, then place in the oven and cook for 15 minutes.

Remove from the oven and leave to cool on the sheet for 5 minutes to harden, then use a spatula to transfer them to a wire rack.

Tip
~ If your children are helping you in the kitchen, get them to break the egg in a small bowl first before it goes in the mixture—this avoids getting stray pieces of shell in your cookies.

MAIDA HEATTER'S BROWNIE CRISPS

Makes about 30

8 tablespoons (1 stick) unsalted butter, plus extra for greasing
2oz dark (85% cocoa solids) chocolate, coarsely chopped
1 teaspoon instant coffee granules
½ cup granulated sugar
1 large free-range egg
½ teaspoon vanilla extract
¼ teaspoon salt
¼ cup all-purpose flour
⅔ cup walnut pieces, chopped medium-fine, but not ground

These have all the goodness of a brownie but they're thin and crisp. Plus they're easily whipped up by hand.

Position a rack in the middle of the oven and preheat it to 350°F. Grease a 15 x 10in baking pan.

Melt the butter in a saucepan over medium heat, allowing it to sizzle and get really hot. Remove from the heat, add the chocolate, and whisk until smooth. Whisk in the instant coffee. Use a rubber spatula to stir in the sugar, followed by the egg and vanilla, then the salt and flour.

Pour the batter into the prepared pan and smooth the top. Sprinkle with the walnuts.

Bake for 15 minutes, turning back to front halfway through.

As soon as they're baked, cut the crisps into 2in squares, then use a wide spatula to transfer them to a rack to cool. Store in a box or plastic container with a tight-fitting lid.

TRULY GOOEY CHOCOLATE AND HAZELNUT COOKIES

Makes 16

¼ cup all-purpose flour

1½ teaspoons baking powder

3½oz milk chocolate, coarsely chopped

3½oz white chocolate, coarsely chopped

3½oz blanched hazelnuts

9oz dark (70% cocoa solids) chocolate

2 large free-range eggs plus 1 large free-range egg yolk

½ cup plus 1 tablespoon granulated sugar

These are from Georgie Fuggle, our amazing recipe tester, who came up with some great recipes herself. These are the ultimate in gooey cookies and so easy to make.

Preheat the oven to 350°F and line three baking sheets with parchment paper.

In a medium bowl combine the flour, baking powder, chopped milk and white chocolates, and the hazelnuts. Set aside.

Melt the dark chocolate in a microwave or heatproof bowl over a pan of barely simmering water, making sure the bowl doesn't touch the water. Remove the bowl from the heat, stir, and set aside to cool.

Whisk the eggs and yolk with the sugar until light and fluffy. Add the dry ingredients and then pour in the cooled chocolate. Stir to combine.

Spoon heaping tablespoons of the mixture onto the prepared baking sheets. Bake for 10 minutes—no longer.

Allow to cool before eating!

ALMOST OREOS

Makes about 20

For the dough
1 cup all-purpose flour
½ teaspoon salt
1 tablespoon cocoa
  powder
⅓ cup superfine sugar
¼ cup confectioners' sugar
1oz dark (70% cocoa solids)
  chocolate, broken
  into pieces
7 tablespoons butter, at room
  temperature

1 extra-large free-range egg yolk
½ teaspoon vanilla
  extract

For the ganache
4½oz white chocolate
3 tablespoons crème fraîche

The contrast of the dark, almost black, Oreo biscuits with their filling of pure white icing is iconic. This recipe takes that idea but uses our vanilla-rich white chocolate to make a velvety ganache filling. Try this one with your children and have fun getting them to make them as perfect and neat as the originals.

Sift together the flour, salt, and cocoa powder into a bowl. Mix together the sugar and confectioners' sugar in a separate bowl. Melt the chocolate in a heatproof bowl over a pan of barely simmering water, making sure the bowl doesn't touch the water, then set aside to cool.

Using an electric beater or hand blender, cream the butter and sugar until light and fluffy. Scrape down the sides of the bowl with a flexible spatula. Add the egg yolk, vanilla extract, and melted chocolate. Beat well to incorporate all the ingredients. Scrape the sides of the bowl again, then add in the dry ingredients. Mix on a slow speed, until a dough forms.

Turn the dough onto a clean work surface and shape it into a cylinder shape about 6in long. Roll the cylinder on the work surface to even it out, then wrap it in plastic wrap and refrigerate for at least 1 hour 30 minutes.

When the dough has rested sufficiently, preheat the oven to 350°F and cover two baking sheets with parchment paper.

To make the ganache, melt the white chocolate in a heatproof bowl over a pan of barely simmering water, making sure the bowl doesn't touch the water. Add the crème fraîche, take off the heat, mix together, and allow to cool for about 15 minutes at room temperature.

Remove the dough from the fridge, unwrap it, and place on a cutting board. Using a sharp knife, slice the cylinder into 40 very thin rounds (⅛in). Place the rounds on the baking sheets and cook them in two batches, each for 12 minutes. Once cooked, leave to cool on the sheets.

Once they have cooled down, turn half the cookies upside down on a baking sheet and put a teaspoonful of ganache in the center of each. Top with the remaining cookies and press gently together so that the ganache spreads until you can see it around the sides. Put the assembled cookies in the fridge in a sealed container. Leave them for at least 30 minutes before eating to allow the ganache to set. They will keep for several days stored in this way.

Tips

~ Cut 20 rounds of the dough and put them on a baking sheet to cook immediately. You can slice the remainder while the first batch is cooking on the baking sheet.

~ If your kitchen is quite warm, cut the cylinder of dough in half and refrigerate one half while you slice the other.

~ It is harder than it seems to keep the dough's perfect cylindrical shape, but there are a few things you can try:

  ~ When wrapping the dough, make sure you twist the plastic wrap fairly tightly from both ends simultaneously, thereby tightening the plastic and resulting in a more even shape.

  ~ Having made sure it is tightly sealed, gently put the rolled up pastry in a plastic container filled with cold water and leave to rest in the fridge. This will help the cylinder keep its shape. Alternatively, it's worth turning the cylinder at regular intervals so that it doesn't flatten on one side under its own weight.

  ~ If you find that, after cooking, the cookies are less than perfectly round, let them cool down slightly, say for about 3 minutes, and carefully cut out circles using a rounded pastry cutter almost the size of each cookie. Allow the cookies to cool down fully and follow the method as described above.

ALLEGRA McEVEDY'S NOT MILLIONAIRE'S SHORTBREAD

For the base
½lb Fairtrade peanuts,
   lightly roasted
2 extra-large free-range eggs
½ cup Fairtrade
   granulated sugar
I teaspoon baking soda
½ teaspoon salt
Splash of peanut/sunflower oil

For the middle
I cup Fairtrade
   superfine sugar
½ cup heavy cream

For the top
7oz maya gold
   or milk chocolate

Makes about 12 good slices

This is a flourless, Fairtrade (hence the title) version of these classic squares of sweetness, which swaps the traditional shortbread layer for a more cookie-like peanutty base. My caramel is gooier than the usual solid fudge middle layer, and the whole thing is topped off with the richness and blend of flavors unique to Maya Gold. I think the words are "naughty but nice," and at least the ethics make you feel better!

Preheat the oven to 350°F. Place the peanuts in a food processor and process to the texture of ground almonds.

Line a small roasting pan or baking sheet about 8in square and 2in deep (or an equivalent-sized rectangular pan is fine too) with parchment paper that has been lightly oiled on both sides. Thoroughly mix together all the ingredients for the base in a bowl, then press evenly into the bottom of the prepared sheet and cook for 30 minutes.

Take out of the oven and immediately use an offset spatula to compress and compact the dough. Leave to cool completely.

Have your sugar and heavy cream weighed out ready. Put a thick-bottomed saucepan on a medium heat and leave it to get hot.

Slowly pour the superfine sugar into the center of the pan so that it forms a mound in the middle. The edges will start to liquify and caramelize. Gently jiggle the pan so that the liquid edges start to eat the grains of sugar. As the island of sugar starts wobbling about on its hidden lake of liquid caramel underneath, gently push the grains of dry sugar down until they are all devoured. If you see that a small patch of it is beginning to burn, stir it as quickly as you can so the heat is dissipated.

Be very calm and gentle, take your time and never leave it alone.

You'll know it's ready when the sugar is all is dissolved and a lovely reddish brown color. Add the heavy cream and stir like mad for a minute. Pour on top of the base and leave to set, either at room temperature or in the fridge if you're in a hurry or in the freezer if you're in a mad panic.

Once the caramel is pretty much solid, melt the chocolate in a heatproof bowl over a pan of barely simmering water, making sure the bowl doesn't touch the water, stirring from time to time (or you can melt it in the microwave). Pour it onto the caramel and level the surface with an offset spatula Leave to set at room temperature—putting chocolate in the fridge is not a good idea.

When the chocolate is set, just lift the whole thing out by pulling up on the paper and cut into squares using a hot knife.

Tips
~ Before you start, make absolutely certain that the pan is clean and there aren't any impurities in the sugar and water solution. Stray bits of food could ruin the caramel.
~ A good way to clean your pan is to fill it with water and put back on the stove over low heat to soak off the caramel.

CHOCOLATE TIFFIN

Makes 24 squares

⅔ cup whole blanched
   almonds
⅔ cup whole blanched
   pistachios
14 tablespoons unsalted butter
½ cup corn syrup
¾lb gingersnaps,
   crushed
½ cup good-quality
   cocoa powder
½ cup golden raisins
11½oz milk chocolate,
   broken into pieces

This recipe was kindly supplied by Rachael Nimento, a good friend of one of the G&B's team here. Rachael has worked in an impressive array of well-known places from The Balmoral Hotel in Edinburgh to The French Laundry in Napa Valley, where she has developed her passion for patisserie. Her Tiffin recipe is a favorite version of this classic and is perfect served up for an afternoon snack!

Preheat the oven to 350°F and gently roast the nuts for about 5 minutes until they are just beginning to change color. Line a 10in square baking pan with parchment paper.

Melt the butter and syrup together in a pan.

Place the crushed gingersnaps, cocoa, nuts, and raisins into a large mixing bowl, or use an electric mixer with the paddle attachment, and mix until well combined. Add the melted butter and syrup to the mixture. Press into the lined pan making it as flat as possible. Put into the fridge for 1½ hours.

Melt the milk chocolate in a microwave or heatproof bowl over a pan of barely simmering water, making sure the bowl doesn't touch the water, stirring from time to time. When almost melted, remove from the heat and continue stirring to melt any remaining lumps.

Remove the chilled tiffin from the fridge and, using an offset spatula, spread half of the melted chocolate over the top of the tiffin and roughly smooth over. Leave for a few minutes until the chocolate is just set and then spread over the remaining chocolate, quickly smooth over with the offset spatula, and then use the tines of a fork to create wave-like patterns. Leave until the wavy layer of chocolate has just set, which will probably take about 5 to 10 minutes. Cut into squares.

Tips

~ This is a good recipe to make in advance: keep it in an airtight container and it will still be delicious 10
   days later.
~ If you don't have a big enough cake pan, use a medium roasting pan; the mixture will mold to
   any shape!
~ To make this taste a little festive, add 1 teaspoon ground spice and the zest of 1 orange to the syrup.

CHOCOLATE-DRIZZLED FRUITY OAT BARS

Makes 12 bars

11 tablespoons unsalted
butter, cubed, plus extra
for greasing
⅓ cup light brown
muscovado sugar
3 tablespoons clear honey
2½ cups steel-cut oats
6oz pack dried berries
3½oz milk chocolate,
cut into chunks

This recipe was given to us by the British actress Donna Air, and we agree, oat bars are a classic and delicious recipe. "They are so simple and taste yummy. I can literally eat them by the bucket load. What I really love about this recipe (apart from the taste, of course, especially because they are drizzled with chocolate!) is that you can adapt it using whatever dried fruits you want. I would recommend dried berries like cranberries or some cherries as they are great superfoods. Apricots would be great too, or even dried pears in autumn... This treat is great for both moms and kids as steel-cut oats are a great source of essential fatty acids, which we all know are necessary for good health. Perfect to have on hand as an 'in between snack.' Enjoy!"

Preheat the oven to 350°F. Lightly grease a 12 x 8 x 1½in non-stick baking pan.

Heat the butter, sugar, and honey gently in a pan, stirring occasionally, until the butter has melted and the sugar has dissolved.

Remove from the heat and stir in the oats, dried fruit, and half the chocolate chunks. Put the mixture into the prepared pan, spread evenly, and bake in the oven for 20 to 25 minutes, until golden brown.

Remove from the oven and allow to cool completely in the pan.

Melt the remaining chocolate in a microwave or heatproof bowl over a pan of barely simmering water, making sure the bowl doesn't touch the water. Drizzle the chocolate over the bars in the pan and leave to cool so the chocolate hardens. Use a knife to cut into 12 bars.

Tip
~ You can store these oat bars in an airtight container for up to 3 days.

WALNUT AND APRICOT CHOCOLATE SLICES

Makes about 12

9oz shortcrust pastry
 (see page 81)
¼ cup plus 2 tablespoons
 smooth apricot jelly
1 cup walnuts
3 extra-large free-range eggs
¾ cup packed brown sugar
4 tablespoons (½ stick)
 unsalted butter, melted
⅔ cup all-purpose flour
4½oz soft/semi-dried
 apricots, chopped small
9oz dark (70% cocoa solids)
 chocolate

As a small child in the mid 70s, I was introduced to the pairing of chocolate and apricots in the form of a Thornton's Apricot Parfait and have been a fan of the combination ever since. Fresh apricots can be so disappointing, often lacking flavor and with a floury textureless form. This recipe combines both a tasty walnut frangipane with a pastry base and a chocolate topping. A great combination of textures and flavors.

Preheat the oven to 350°F and line an 8 x 12in cake pan with parchment paper. Roll out the pastry just a little bigger than the base of the cake pan to allow for some shrinkage as the pastry cooks, and use to line the base of the pan. Bake the pastry for 15 to 20 minutes or until it's a deep golden brown. When cooked, leave to cool, still in the cake pan, then spread the jelly over the pastry.

Chop the walnuts very finely in a food processor. Whisk the eggs and sugar until light and fluffy, then fold in the melted butter along with the sifted flour. Blend in the walnuts.

Pour this mixture over the pastry and spread out evenly. Return to the oven and bake for 25 to 30 minutes, until firm. Remove and leave to cool. Distribute the chopped apricots over the cake.

Melt the chocolate in a microwave or heatproof bowl over a pan of barely simmering water, making sure the bowl doesn't touch the water. Using a large spoon or spatula, cover the cake with an even layer of chocolate.

Allow the chocolate to set before removing the cake from the pan and placing it onto a cutting board. Use a sharp serrated knife to cut the cake into 12 or more slices.

Tips
~ *Feel free to increase or reduce the amount of apricot jelly and/or apricots. If you can only get ahold of hard dried apricots, you can always cover them in water and leave overnight to plump up.*
~ *To achieve a good contrast of textures, your pastry needs to be crisp and firm. Do bake it fully at the outset as it will not bake much more the second time it goes in the oven.*

ANITA'S WONDERFUL WHOOPIE PIES

Makes about 10

For the pies
9 tablespoons butter
5½oz dark (70% cocoa solids) chocolate
1 cup plus 2 tablespoons sugar
3 extra-large free-range eggs
1 teaspoon vanilla extract
2 cups flour
3 tablespoons good-quality cocoa powder
½ teaspoon baking powder

For the filling
3½ tablespoons unsalted butter
2 tablespoons 1% milk
½ teaspoon vanilla extract
2 cups confectioners' sugar

For those of you who have never encountered a whoopie pie, it originates from the Amish of Pennsylvania and is traditionally made up of two soft cookies sandwiched together with a marshmallow filling and is about the size of a hamburger. However, my esteemed Danish/British hybrid colleague Anita Kinniburgh, who is a master baker, has her own take on them. They are smaller, more buttery/chocolatey, and are sandwiched with a buttercream icing. Some say she is a genius; I just call her darling.

Preheat the oven to 350°F and line two baking sheets with parchment paper.

Melt the butter and chocolate in a heatproof bowl over a pan of barely simmering water, making sure the bowl doesn't touch the water. Remove from the heat and allow to cool slightly.

Whisk the sugar, eggs, and vanilla in a separate bowl for about 3 minutes or until light, fluffy, and pale in color, then fold in the chocolate mixture.

Sift the flour, cocoa, and baking powder together and fold into the mixture.

Place tablespoons of the mixture onto the baking sheets (the mixture should make about 20 halves) and bake for 10 to 12 minutes. Remove from the oven and allow to cool.

For the buttercream icing, cream the ingredients together (initially with a wooden spoon—if you start with an electric beater, you may disappear in a cloud of confectioners' sugar).

When the pies have cooled, pair them up and apply a layer of butter icing to one of the flatter sides and sandwich them together.

Tip
~ *For those who would like to try something more like the original, make the hot meringue from either the Baked Alaska (page 92) or the Chocolate Meringue Pie (page 167) and use that as a filling.*

ULTIMATE CHOCOLATE BROWNIES

Makes 24

10½oz unsalted butter
10½oz dark (70% cocoa
   solids) chocolate,
   broken into pieces
5 extra-large free-range eggs
2¼ cups granulated sugar
1 tablespoon vanilla
   extract
1⅔ cups all-purpose flour
1 teaspoon salt

An Ultimate Chocolate Recipes book would not be complete without an Ultimate Chocolate Brownie recipe. I searched high and low and tested many recipes but came back to the version we have in our first book (although I've taken the cherries out of this one). Incredibly easy to make, decadently chocolatey, not too sweet, a light crust outside and beautifully moist within, but with enough salt to cut through the richness.

Preheat the oven to 350°F. Line a 13 x 10in baking pan at least 2¼in deep with parchment paper.

Melt the butter and chocolate together in a heatproof bowl over a saucepan of barely simmering water, making sure the bowl doesn't touch the water. Beat the eggs, sugar, and vanilla extract together in a bowl until the mixture is thick and creamy and coats the back of a spoon. Once the butter and the chocolate have melted, remove from the heat and beat in the egg mixture. Sift the flour and salt together, then add them to the mixture and continue to beat until smooth.

Pour into the baking pan, ensuring the mixture is evenly distributed. Bake in the oven for 20 to 25 minutes or until the whole top has formed a light brown crust that has started to crack. This giant brownie should not wobble, but should remain gooey on the inside.

Leave it to cool for about 20 minutes before cutting into large squares while still in the pan. The parchment paper should peel off easily.

Tips
~ Add a handful of your favorite nuts or dried fruits to the mixture before you transfer it to the baking pan. You can cut them up or leave them whole, as you prefer.
~ Always taste the mixture raw (use caution due to the slight risk of Salmonella or other food-borne diseases when consuming raw eggs) to check for your preferred vanilla and salt levels, ensuring you leave some to bake, of course.

CHOCOLATE AND RASPBERRY CHEESECAKE BROWNIES

Makes 16

For the brownie mix
10oz (2½ sticks) unsalted butter, plus extra for greasing
6oz dark (70% cocoa solids) chocolate
1¾ cups unrefined golden baker's sugar
½ cup all-purpose flour
Pinch of salt
5 large free-range eggs
2 teaspoons vanilla extract
3½oz white chocolate, broken into small pieces

For the cheesecake mix
1½ cups cream cheese
⅓ cup unrefined golden baker's sugar
1 teaspoon vanilla extract
2 large free-range eggs
6oz fresh raspberries

A lifelong fan of the brand, Felicity Hood developed this recipe for our consumer competition to encompass her two favorite things—raspberries and chocolate! A regular holder of dinner parties, she often delights her friends with this recipe; it looks absolutely stunning and tastes sensational, so is a real crowd pleaser.

Preheat the oven to 350°F. Grease and line a 8in square brownie pan.

To make the brownie mixture, melt the butter and chocolate in a heatproof bowl over a pan of barely simmering water, making sure the bowl doesn't touch the water. Stir until completely melted and combined. Remove from the heat and set aside to cool.

Combine the sugar, flour, and salt in a large mixing bowl, pour over the cooled chocolate, and mix until smooth. Beat the eggs separately before adding to the mixing bowl along with the vanilla extract and the white chocolate.

Blend together until you create a shiny chocolatey mixture. Pour this into the prepared pan.

Next make the cheesecake mixture. Whisk the cream cheese, sugar, vanilla extract, and eggs until smooth and creamy. Pour this carefully over the brownie mix, trying to create an even layer.

Use a fork to drag the cheesecake mix through the brownie mix to create a marbled effect. Drop the raspberries into the pan. Try to ensure that all the raspberries are almost fully pushed into the mixture.

Cook in the preheated oven for about 35 to 40 minutes. After 30 minutes remove the pan and check to see if the brownies are set but still have a slight wobble to them; return to the oven if they need a little longer. Leave to cool in the pan, covered with foil.

Once cooled, take the yummy brownies out of the pan, cut into 16 pieces, and serve to your lucky guests.

JUDGES BAKERY'S CHOCOLATE CUPCAKES

Makes 24

1½oz dark (70% cocoa solids) chocolate

2 tablespoons whole milk

1 cup plus two tablespoons unsalted butter

1¼ cups superfine sugar

4 extra-large free-range eggs

1⅔ cups all-purpose flour

⅓ cup good-quality cocoa powder

1½ teaspoons baking powder

1 teaspoon vanilla extract

For the frosting

7oz dark (70% cocoa solids) chocolate

4 cups confectioners' sugar, sifted

14 tablespoons unsalted butter, softened

⅓ cup whole milk

Green & Black's founders, Craig Sams and Josephine Fairley, have gone on to open an award-winning artisan bakery and one-stop organic and local food store in the Old Town in Hastings, on the south coast of the UK, where they moved after leaving Green & Black's birthplace (Portobello Road). Naturally, there's only one chocolate they'd consider using in any chocolate recipe—including these cupcakes, which fly out the door...

Preheat the oven to 350°F. Line two 12-hole muffin pans with cupcake liners.

Melt the chocolate in a microwave or heatproof bowl over a pan of barely simmering water, making sure the bowl doesn't touch the water. Remove from the heat and allow to cool slightly.

Beat the butter, sugar, and vanilla extract together with an electric mixer until light and fluffy.

Add the eggs a little at a time, beating to combine between each addition, then fold in the cooled melted chocolate. Sift the flour, cocoa powder, and baking powder together then gently fold into the mixture.

Transfer the mixture to a piping bag fitted with a large nozzle and pipe into the paper liners to within ½in of the top.

Place the pans in the preheated oven and bake for about 15 minutes until risen and golden. Remove from the oven and cool the cakes in their liners on a wire rack.

For the frosting, melt the chocolate as above. Remove from the heat and allow to cool.

Beat the confectioners' sugar and butter together with an electric mixer on medium until the mixture comes together. Combine the milk with the cooled melted chocolate. Add this slowly to the creamed mixture. Once combined, increase the mixer speed to high, and mix until light and fluffy. (You may need to add a little extra milk to get the required spreading consistency).

Once the cupcakes have cooled, ice them with your gorgeous frosting.

Tip

~ Decorate each cake with shards of chocolate for a striking effect.

PRIMROSE BAKERY'S PEANUT BUTTER CUPCAKES

Makes 12 regular cupcakes

5 tablespoons unsalted butter, at room temperature
½ cup smooth peanut butter
1 cup dark brown sugar
2 extra-large free-range eggs
1 teaspoon good-quality vanilla extract
1 cup all-purpose flour
1 teaspoon baking powder
Pinch of salt
¼ cup milk

For the frosting
¼ cup heavy cream
2 tablespoons unsalted butter
10½oz milk chocolate, broken into pieces
½ teaspoon vanilla extract
peanut butter or chocolate chips, to garnish

This is a fairly dense and rich cupcake. You can make these for special holidays or gatherings—but we warn you, they are too good to eat just a few times a year! Peanut butter chips such as Reese's Pieces are delicious and fun toppings for these cupcakes, but chocolate chips can be just as festive, too.

Preheat the oven to 350°F. Line a 12-hole regular-size muffin pan with cupcake liners.

Cream the butter, peanut butter, and sugar until well blended. Add the eggs one at a time, mixing for a few minutes after each addition, and then stir in the vanilla extract.

Combine the flour, baking powder, and salt in a separate bowl. Add one-third of the flour to the creamed mixture and beat well. Pour in one-third of the milk and beat again. Repeat these steps until all the flour mixture and milk have been incorporated.

Carefully spoon the mixture into the cupcake liners, filling them to about two-thirds full. Bake for about 20 minutes until slightly raised and golden brown. Insert a skewer in the center of one of the cakes to check that they are cooked—it should come out clean.

Remove from the oven and leave the cakes in their pan for about 10 minutes before carefully placing on a wire rack to cool. Once completely cool, top with milk chocolate frosting (see below). Top with peanut butter or milk chocolate chips.

For the frosting, add the heavy cream and butter to a saucepan over very low heat. Stir the mixture continuously and do not let it come to a boil or it will burn. As soon as the butter has completely melted, remove from the heat and add the chocolate. Allow the chocolate to melt in the pan, which may take up to 10 minutes, during which time stir the mixture continuously. If any pieces remain, return the pan to very low heat and melt the chocolate again. Add the vanilla extract and stir again.

If the frosting is too runny to use, allow it to remain at room temperature for a while, then beat again just before you start to decorate your cupcakes. Any unused frosting can be stored in a container in the fridge.

WHITE CHOCOLATE AND BLACKBERRY CUPCAKES

Makes 12

10 tablespoons unsalted
  butter, softened
⅔ cup superfine sugar
3 large free-range eggs
1 teaspoon vanilla extract
1½ cups self-rising flour
1 to 2 splashes of milk,
  if needed
3½oz white chocolate,
  coarsely chopped

For the frosting
8oz (2 sticks) unsalted butter,
  softened
3¾ cups confectioners' sugar
4½oz blackberries,
  lightly crushed (reserve
  12 whole ones for
  decoration—see tip)

Georgie Fuggle, nee Footitt, has gone onto great things since her time at Green & Black's, including opening her own pop-up restaurant with close friend Alice. Not only did she help us by testing many of the recipes in this book, but also contributed some of her own. I love this one as it balances the sweetness of the white chocolate cake with a tart blackberry icing. Joe, our finance analyst, likes them because he thinks they are pretty.

Preheat the oven to 375°F. Line a 12-hole muffin pan with the prettiest of cupcake liners.

Using an electric stand or hand-held mixer, cream the butter and sugar until light and fluffy.

Add in the eggs one by one, beating between each addition to combine. Mix in the vanilla extract.

Add in the flour and combine. If the mixture seems too dry, splash in a little milk: the mixture should be of a dropping consistency. Stir in the white chocolate pieces.

Pour the mixture into the prepared liners about two-thirds of the way up. Bake for 15 to 20 minutes or until well risen and springy to the touch. Leave to cool completely before frosting.

For the frosting, make sure the butter is really soft and then use an electric stand or hand-held mixer to whisk it with the confectioners' sugar until light and smooth. Whisk through the blackberries. Transfer to a piping bag and pipe luxurious amounts onto the top of each cooled cupcake.

Tip
~ Decorate each cake with a blackberry.

THE HUMMINGBIRD BAKERY'S GINGER CHOCOLATE CUPCAKES

3 tablespoons unsalted butter, softened
¾ cup superfine sugar
¾ cup all-purpose flour
2 tablespoons good-quality cocoa powder
1 teaspoon ground ginger
½ tablespoon baking powder
⅓ cup whole milk
1 large free-range egg

For the frosting
7 tablespoons unsalted butter, softened
2 cups confectioners' sugar
⅓ cup cocoa powder
3 tablespoons whole milk
3½oz dark chocolate with ginger

Makes 10-12 cupcakes

Ginger and chocolate are sympathetic bedfellows, working in all sorts of combinations. Our friends at The Hummingbird Bakery have used the ground spice in the cake then used our dark bar with crystallized ginger in the icing. This recipe shows off two different forms of ginger and how they complement each other. A case of the whole being greater than the sum of its parts.

Preheat the oven to 350°F. Line a 12-hole muffin pan with cupcake liners.

Using an electric stand or hand-held mixer on a slow speed, whisk together the butter, sugar, flour, cocoa powder, ginger, and baking powder. Mix until there are no large lumps of butter remaining.

Whisk the milk and egg together in a separate bowl and pour half the liquid into the creamed ingredients and mix on a slow speed until all is combined. Increase the speed to medium to ensure a smooth batter. Scrape down the sides and bottom of the bowl to ensure everything is well mixed in. Add the remaining liquid and mix on a medium-high speed to give a smooth batter with all the ingredients well incorporated.

Melt the chocolate in a microwave or heatproof bowl over a pan of barely simmering water, making sure the bowl doesn't touch the water. Once the chocolate is melted and smooth, stir to cool it down and then whisk it into the cupcake batter. Scoop the batter into the prepared cupcake liners, filling them about two-thirds full. Bake for 20 to 25 minutes or until well risen and springy to the touch. Leave to cool completely before frosting.

For the frosting, use an electric stand or hand-held mixer to whisk together the butter, confectioners' sugar, and cocoa powder until there are no large lumps of butter remaining and all the ingredients are well incorporated. Add the milk on a slow speed, and then increase the speed to high and beat for about 1 minute until the frosting is light and fluffy.

Coarsely chop the ginger chocolate. Try not to have too many large pieces, but also not too fine, as you want to have small pieces of chocolate coating the top of the cupcake to give some texture and crunch. Hand frost the cooled cupcakes with the chocolate frosting and then coat the tops of the cupcakes with the chopped ginger chocolate.

THE HUMMINGBIRD BAKERY'S DARK CHOCOLATE CUPCAKES

3 tablespoons unsalted butter, softened
¾ cup superfine sugar
¾ cup all-purpose flour
2 tablespoons cocoa powder
½ tablespoon baking powder
⅓ cup whole milk
1 medium free-range egg
2oz dark (85% cocoa solids) chocolate

For the frosting
7 tablespoons unsalted butter, softened
2½ cups confectioners' sugar
½ cup cocoa powder
¼ cup whole milk
2oz dark (85% cocoa solids) chocolate
2oz dark (70% cocoa solids) chocolate

Makes 10-12 cupcakes

Lots of dark chocolate plus lots of cocoa powder plus lots of butter equals lots of flavor. Thank you, The Hummingbird Bakery.

Preheat the oven to 350°F and line a 12-hole muffin pan with cupcake liners.

Using an electric stand or hand-held mixer on a slow speed, whisk together the butter, sugar, flour, cocoa powder, and baking powder. Mix until there are no large lumps of butter remaining.

Whisk the milk and egg together in a separate bowl and pour half the liquid into the creamed ingredients and mix on a slow speed until all is combined. Increase the speed to medium to ensure a smooth batter. Scrape down the sides and bottom of the bowl to ensure everything is well mixed in. Add the remaining liquid and mix on medium-high speed to give a smooth batter with all the ingredients well incorporated.

Melt the chocolate in a microwave or heatproof bowl over a pan of barely simmering water, making sure the bowl doesn't touch the water. Once the chocolate is melted and smooth, stir to cool it and then whisk it into the batter. Scoop the batter into the prepared cupcake liners, filling them about two-thirds of the way to the top. Bake for 20 to 25 minutes or until well risen and springy to the touch. Remove from the oven and leave to cool completely on a wire rack before frosting.

To make the frosting, use an electric or hand-held mixer to whisk the butter, confectioners' sugar, and cocoa powder until there are no large lumps of butter remaining and all the ingredients are well incorporated. Add the milk on a slow speed, and then increase the speed to high and beat for about 1 minute until the frosting is light and fluffy.

Melt the two dark chocolates as before. Stir the chocolate to cool it down slightly and then pour ¼ of it into the chocolate frosting, mixing continuously until it is evenly dispersed through the frosting.

Hand frost the cooled cupcakes with the chocolate frosting and place them in the fridge for 5 to 10 minutes until the frosting is set and cold.

Dip the frosting very gently into the remaining melted chocolate and leave to set. The coating of chocolate will set, leaving a hard chocolate shell on the soft frosting.

CHOCOLATE CHIP SCONES

Makes 6 to 8

1¾ cups all-purpose flour,
  plus extra for dusting
Pinch of salt
¼ cup superfine sugar
1 teaspoon baking powder
3 tablespoons unsalted
  butter, cubed
3½oz dark (70% cocoa solids)
  chocolate, chopped into
  chocolate-chip sized pieces
½ cup 1% milk, to mix
1 free-range egg, beaten

I can already hear the traditionalists amongst you shouting, "Keep those pesky chocolate chips away from my beloved scones (surely pronounced skon and not skohn)!" Well, no, I won't. Throw in a bar (chopped up) into your favorite scone mixture or use the recipe below and bake in the usual manner. I think you'll find that they are at least as good as the non-chocolate variety and are delicious smothered with the customary home-made jelly and clotted cream.

Preheat the oven to 425°F.

Sift all the dry ingredients together in a large wide bowl. Add the butter cubes, toss in the flour mix, and then rub in until the mixture resembles coarse breadcrumbs. Stir in the chopped chocolate and make a well in the center. Add the milk to the dry ingredients and mix to form a soft dough. Turn onto a floured board.

Knead the dough lightly, just enough to shape into a round. Roll out to a thickness of about 1in and cut into scones using a 2½in round cutter. Place the scones on a baking sheet—no need to grease.

Brush the tops with beaten egg and bake for 10 to 12 minutes until golden brown on top. Cool on a wire rack.

CHOCOLATE CARDAMOM MUFFINS

Makes 12 muffins

2oz milk chocolate
5½oz dark (70% cocoa solids) chocolate, chopped
2 cups all-purpose flour
2 teaspoons baking powder
½ teaspoon baking soda
2 level tablespoons good-quality cocoa

¾ cup superfine sugar
Seeds of 3-4 cardamom pods, ground finely
1¼ cups whole milk
⅓ cup vegetable oil
1 extra-large free-range egg

I must make a confession here: I don't really like muffins. I also insist on calling them oversized cupcakes, because a true muffin is a bread item you toast and serve, ideally, with some ham, poached egg, and hollandaise sauce. I don't know where I was when this baked good suddenly adopted the prefix "English," but I refuse to use it. Anyway, I challenged a cake enthusiast colleague, Gail, to come up with a chocolate muffin I would enjoy. She made a few versions, but it was the one where she added cardamom, a spice that marries particularly well with chocolate, that got my vote. Out of respect, I finished the whole thing.

Preheat the oven to 400°F. Line a 12-space muffin pan with muffin cups.

Melt the milk chocolate in the microwave or in a bowl over a pan of simmering water, making sure the bowl doesn't touch the water. Leave to cool.

Mix all the dry ingredients together in a large mixing bowl.

Mix the cooled milk chocolate with the milk, vegetable oil, and egg in a separate bowl. Add the dry mixture to the milk chocolate mixture, and combine but don't overmix.

Divide the mixture evenly among the 12 muffin cups and bake in the oven for 20 minutes or until risen and springy.

CHOCOLATE CHIP MADELEINES

Makes 24

10 tablespoons unsalted
  butter, plus extra
  for greasing
2 tablespoons of your
  favorite honey
3 extra-large free-range eggs
⅔ cup superfine sugar
1 cup self-rising flour,
  plus extra for dusting
3½oz dark (70% cocoa
  solids) chocolate, chopped
  into very small pieces

This recipe is (very slightly) adapted from the second St. John restaurant cookbook, *Beyond Nose to Tail* (if you don't already have both the St. John books, buy them now as not only are the recipes brilliant but the turn of phrase is a joy). I would recommend you buy one or two 12-hole madeleine pans for this, if you don't already have one, as once you've made these you'll be sure to make them again. You can serve the first batch while the second batch is in the oven; you'll need both.

Melt the butter and honey in a small saucepan and simmer until syrupy—about 8 minutes. Pour into a bowl and set aside to cool. Don't worry if the mixture splits slightly.

Using an electric stand or hand-held mixer, whisk the eggs and sugar together for around 8 minutes or until the mixture has tripled in volume.

Fold in the flour then the butter mixture and leave until cold. Stir the chopped chocolate into the cake mixture. Rest in the fridge for a couple of hours.

Preheat the oven to 375°F. Butter and flour the madeleine molds. Put a teaspoonful of mixture into each mold and bake for about 15 minutes or until just firm to the touch and golden brown.

Best served warm.

SACHERTORTE

Serves 10

For the torte
Melted butter, for greasing
9oz dark (70% cocoa solids)
  chocolate
2 extra-large free-range
  egg yolks
3½oz granulated sugar
5 extra-large free-range
  egg whites
1¼ cups ground almonds
1½ teaspoons freshly
  ground coffee
½ teaspoon salt

For the icing
3½oz dark (70% cocoa solids)
  chocolate
3 tablespoons (⅓ stick)
  unsalted butter

An ex-colleague and good friend, Jamie Ewan, asked me to make her a chocolate cake for her wedding. Despite never having made one before (a wedding cake, that is, not a chocolate cake) and that I was arriving back from the US a day before her wedding, how could I refuse her? I read books on how to bake big cakes and bought all sorts of pans and equipment (note to self: stop buying more kitchen stuff). However, the most important thing was to get a chocolate cake recipe that was properly moist and chocolatey. I experimented with a sachertorte recipe and ended up reducing the sugar and adding even more chocolate – this seems to be my answer to everything.

Preheat the oven to 350°F. Brush a 10in springform cake pan with melted butter, then line it with parchment paper.

To make the torte, melt the chocolate in a microwave or heatproof bowl suspended over a saucepan of barely simmering water, making sure the bowl doesn't touch the water. Set aside to cool.

In a bowl, whisk the egg yolks and sugar until the mixture is thick and creamy.

In a clean bowl whisk the egg whites until stiff peaks form.

Add the ground almonds, coffee, salt, and melted chocolate to the egg yolk mixture and stir well. Gently fold in the egg whites and pour into the prepared pan.

Bake for 55 minutes, covering the cake with foil after 40 minutes to prevent the top from burning. Check that a wooden skewer inserted into the center comes out clean (but with a few crumbs attached) and remove the cake from the oven. Release the springform ring and leave the cake on the base to cool on a wire rack.

To make the icing, melt the chocolate as above. Add the butter and stir until it has the consistency of thick pouring cream.

Pour the icing evenly over the cake, smoothing it over the top and sides using the back of a teaspoon. Leave to set.

ARIANNA'S CHOCOLATE CINNAMON ROLLS

Makes 16

For the dough

3⅓ cups strong bread flour,
  plus extra for dusting
½ cup golden baker's sugar
2½ teaspoons dried,
  fast-acting yeast
1¼ teaspoons salt
¾ cup whole milk
3 tablespoons unsalted butter
1 extra-large free-range egg
1 vanilla bean, split and
  seeds scraped

For the filling

⅔ cup light brown
  muscovado sugar
2½ tablespoons
  ground cinnamon
8 tablespoons (1 stick) unsalted
  butter, at room temperature
5½oz dark (70 % cocoa solids)
  chocolate, finely chopped

For the cinnamon sauce

2 tablespoons unsalted butter,
  plus extra for greasing
¼ cup light brown
  muscovado sugar
Pinch of salt
½ teaspoon cinnamon

"I have known the basic version of this recipe by heart for as long as I can remember. My mother, who is Norwegian, has been making these rolls for every significant family event since she learned them from her mother. When I was shown how to make them as a little girl, always by eye as the recipe had never been written down, I felt so grown up—as if I was being trusted with the most amazing family secret. I have played around with and tweaked the recipe over the years until I perfected my unique version of my childhood favorite. When my mother finally admitted my rolls were better than hers, it was one of my proudest moments as a chef! To me, these rolls are a symbol of family, celebrations, and the start of my love of baking which ultimately led me to become a pastry chef and own my own bakery in London."

To make the dough, place the flour, sugar, yeast, and salt in a medium bowl and stir to combine. Set aside.

Gently heat the milk and butter together until just warmed and the butter has melted.

Using an electric mixer with a paddle attachment, pour the warm milk and butter into the mixer bowl along with the egg and seeds from the vanilla bean, then add half of the dry ingredients and gently mix until combined.

Slowly add the remaining dry ingredients and mix until the flour has been fully incorporated and the dough is sticking to the sides of the bowl. If the dough is really sticky, add more flour, 1 tablespoon at a time, until the dough comes away from the sides of the bowl and starts to form a ball.

Turn the dough onto a floured work surface and knead for about 6 minutes until the dough is firm and elastic. Alternatively, switch to the dough hook on your stand mixer and knead the dough in the bowl for 4 minutes.

Place the dough in a large bowl, loosely cover with plastic wrap, and place a damp kitchen towel over the bowl. Put in a warm, dark place and leave the dough to rise for 1½ to 2 hours, until it has doubled in volume.

Meanwhile, prepare the ingredients for the sauce. Melt the butter, sugar, salt, and cinnamon together and pour into the bottom of a greased pan measuring 9 x 13in. Set aside.

For the filling, mix together the brown sugar and cinnamon and set aside. Chop the chocolate and set aside.

Once the dough has doubled in volume, remove it from the bowl and smooth out onto a well-floured surface. Roll out into a large rectangle, roughly 14 x 18in.

Spread the room temperature butter evenly onto the dough rectangle to within ½in of the edge on all sides. Sprinkle the sugar and cinnamon mixture over the buttered area and then scatter with chunks of chocolate, aiming for even coverage.

Starting with a long edge, carefully roll the dough, tucking it in firmly as you go, until you reach the opposite edge. Using a serrated knife, cut the "log" in the middle, then into quarters, and then into sixteenths to ensure the rolls are uniform in size.

Place the rolls in the pan with the cinnamon sauce, leaving a ½-in gap between each one. Place a damp kitchen towel over the pan and allow the rolls to rise a second time by leaving for 45 minutes in a warm, dark place.

Meanwhile, preheat the oven to 350°F.

Bake the rolls in the preheated oven until they are puffed up and golden brown. Test by pressing lightly on one of the rolls: if it doesn't feel soft inside, the rolls are cooked.

Allow to cool for at least 30 minutes in the pan. Then, using a baking sheet or large plate that will cover the entire pan, very carefully but swiftly invert the pan. Be sure to use oven mitts because the sauce will be very hot.

Delicious warm or cold.

FARMHOUSE CHOCOLATE BANANA BREAD

Makes 1 loaf

1¾ cups self-rising flour
Pinch of salt
8 tablespoons (1 stick) butter
  at room temperature
¾ cup superfine sugar
2 extra-large free-range
  eggs, beaten
2 very ripe bananas
3 tablespoons milk
3½oz dark (70% or 85%
  cocoa solids) chocolate,
  chopped into very small
  pieces

Charmaine is an avid fan of the brand and sent us this amazing banana bread recipe, which she has adapted to incorporate our chocolate. The result is a deliciously moist loaf cake, lightly flecked with dark chocolate. If that doesn't feel decadent enough, smother with a layer of butter.

Preheat the oven to 350°F and line a 9 x 5in loaf pan.

Sift the flour and salt.

Cream the butter and sugar in a food processor. Add the eggs, bananas, and milk and mix thoroughly. Next add the flour, but stop mixing as soon as the ingredients come together.

Fold half of the chopped chocolate into the mixture. This must be done using a spoon—do not use a food processor for this.

Pour the mixture into the prepared pan, sprinkle the rest of the chocolate on top of the mixture, and push the pieces in slightly.

Bake in the center of the oven for between 45 minutes and 1 hour or until a skewer inserted into the middle comes out clean.

Tip

~ When mixing the wet and dry ingredients, do not work the mixture too much as that will release the gluten in the flour and make for a heavier texture. For this reason, stop when the mixture has just come together.

ALL-IN-ONE SPICED CHOCOLATE LOAF

Makes 1 loaf

2oz dark (70% cocoa solids) chocolate
¾ cup all-purpose flour
1 cup confectioners' sugar
1 teaspoon ground cinnamon
1 teaspoon ground mixed spice (use a mixture of allspice, cinnamon, and nutmeg)
2 teaspoons baking powder
12 tablespoons (1½ sticks) unsalted butter at room temperature, plus extra for greasing
4 extra-large free-range eggs
3½oz dark chocolate with ginger

Even though Denise Rowe, a long-time fan of the brand, lives on the beach, winters bring lots of bracing walks. This dense, slightly spiced chocolate loaf is her ideal way to warm up post-walk, served alongside a cup of tea or coffee.

Preheat the oven 350°F and butter a 9in loaf pan.

Melt the dark chocolate in a microwave or heatproof bowl over a pan of barely simmering water, making sure the bowl doesn't touch the water. Set aside to cool.

Blend the flour, sugar, spices, and baking powder. This is easiest in a food processor, or you can use a hand-held electric mixer.

Add the butter, cooled, melted chocolate, and the eggs and blend until evenly mixed.

Pour the mixture into the loaf pan and bake for about 35 minutes or until a skewer inserted in the middle comes out clean.

Remove from the pan and cool on a wire rack.

Meanwhile, melt the ginger chocolate bar using the same method and drizzle over the cooled cake.

Tip
~ You don't, of course, have to use ginger chocolate for the drizzle. Dark, milk, or white chocolate would also be good.

ANNIE BELL'S GUILT-FREE CHOCOLATE CAKE

Makes 1 x 8in cake

For the cake

4 extra-large free-range eggs, separated
¾ cup golden superfine sugar
3 tablespoons good-quality cocoa powder, sifted
1⅓ cups ground almonds
1 teaspoon baking powder, sifted
Butter, for greasing

For the filling

18oz (about 4¼ cups) tubs of ricotta, drained
3 tablespoons honey
¼ cup coarsely grated dark (70 to 85% cocoa solids) chocolate

There are any number of occasions when you might want to call on this chocolate cake, which, with no butter or cream, is everyone's best friend. It keeps well for several days in the fridge—the liquid in the ricotta seeps into the sponge and keeps it moist.

Preheat the oven to 400°F and butter an 8in cake pan with sides 3½in deep and a removable bottom.

Stiffly whisk the egg whites in a medium bowl—a hand-held electric beater is ideal. Whisk together the egg yolks and sugar in a large bowl until pale and creamy. Fold the egg whites into the egg mixture in thirds, then fold in the cocoa, the ground almonds, and baking powder.

Transfer the cake mixture to the prepared pan, smooth the surface, and bake it for 35 minutes until the sponge has begun to shrink from the sides and a skewer inserted into the center comes out clean. Run a knife around the edge of the cake and leave it to cool in the pan.

For the filling, place the ricotta and honey in a food processor and blend until smooth (if you do this by hand, it will remain grainy). Remove the collar from the cake, but you can leave it on the bottom for ease of serving. Slit the cake in half, taking into account the height in the center of the cake. Reserving a couple of tablespoons of the ricotta cream, spread the rest over the bottom and sandwich with the top half. Spread the reserved cream in a thin layer over the surface of the cake and scatter over the grated chocolate, which should conceal all but the very edge of the cream. Set aside in a cool place.

If keeping the cake longer than a few hours, cover, chill, and bring it back up to room temperature for 30 to 60 minutes before serving.

ROSE LEVY BERANBAUM'S CHOCOLATE LAYER CAKE

Serves 16

¾ cup cocoa powder
¾ cup boiling water
3½oz dark (70% cocoa
  solids) chocolate,
  broken into pieces
4 large free-range eggs
⅓ cup water
1 tablespoon vanilla extract
2½ cups self-rising flour
2 cups superfine sugar
4 teaspoons baking powder
1 teaspoon salt
8oz (2 sticks) unsalted butter
3½ tablespoons oil

**For the dreamy creamy white
chocolate frosting
  (makes 1½lb—enough to
  cover the cake perfectly)**
9oz white chocolate,
  chopped
1½ cups cream cheese
6 tablespoons (¾ stick)
  unsalted butter, softened
¾oz crème fraîche

This deep chocolate cake is filled and frosted with a stunningly luscious contrast of ivory buttercream, flecked with little dots of vanilla bean.

Line two 9 x 2in cake pans with parchment paper. At least 20 minutes before baking, position an oven rack in the lower third of the oven and preheat the oven to 325°F.

In a medium bowl, whisk the cocoa and boiling water until smooth. Cover with plastic wrap to prevent separation and cool to room temperature (about an hour). To speed cooling, place the bowl in the fridge then return it to room temperature before proceeding.

Melt the chocolate in a microwave or heatproof bowl over a pan of barely simmering water, making sure the bowl doesn't touch the water. Stir until completely melted and set aside to cool.

In another bowl, whisk the eggs, water, and vanilla just until lightly combined.

Using an electric beater, mix the flour, sugar, baking powder, and salt on low speed for 30 seconds. Add the butter, oil, and the cocoa mixture. Mix on low speed until the dry ingredients are moistened. Raise the speed to medium and beat for 1½ minutes. Scrape down the sides. Gradually add the egg mixture in two batches, beating for 30 seconds after each addition to incorporate the ingredients and strengthen the structure. Scrape down the sides and finally pour in the melted chocolate.

Scrape the batter into the prepared pans and smooth the surfaces. Bake for 30 to 40 minutes or until a skewer inserted near the centers comes out clean and the cakes spring back when pressed lightly. The cakes should start to shrink from the sides of the pans only after removal from the oven.

Let the cakes cool in their pans on a rack for 10 minutes and then transfer to a wire rack. To prevent splitting, turn the cakes so that the top sides are up, and cool completely before icing (see below).

For the frosting, melt the chocolate in a heatproof bowl over a pan of barely simmering water, making sure the bowl doesn't touch the water. Stir until almost completely melted. Remove the bowl from the heat and allow the chocolate to cool so that it's no longer warm but still fluid.

Process the cream cheese, butter, and crème fraîche in a food processor for a few seconds until smooth and creamy. Scrape down the sides and add the cooled, melted chocolate. Pulse a few times until it is smooth and fully incorporated.

When the cake is completely cool, spread a little buttercream on a 9in cardboard round or a serving plate and set one layer on top, rounded side down. Slide a few wide strips of wax paper or parchment under the cake to keep the rim of the plate clean if using the plate.

Evenly spread a third of the frosting on top and set the second layer on top, rounded side down. Cover the top and sides with the remaining frosting.

Tips
~ This cake can be made without the 3½oz dark chocolate; the result will be lighter but not quite as chocolatey!
~ If desired, level the rounded tops of the cake layers using a long serrated knife.
~ If refrigerating the cake, let it come to room temperature before serving.

HEARTACHE CHOCOLATE CAKE

Serves 14

2 small eggplants
10½oz dark (70% cocoa solids) chocolate, broken into small pieces
½ cup good-quality cocoa powder, plus extra for dusting

⅓ cup ground almonds
3 extra-large free-range eggs
½ cup honey
2 tablespoons baking powder
¼ teaspoon salt
1 tablespoon brandy
Oil, for brushing

This unusual cake is from Harry Eastwood's book _Red Velvet Chocolate Heartache_. It is more healthy than your average chocolate cake with eggplants, honey, and almonds replacing the flour, sugar, and fat. Harry remarks, "This cake is sad. It's dark and drizzling down the window panes. She puffs her chest in hope when she goes into the oven; she then breaks, like a chest heaving a sob. This is why eggplant (the Eeyore of the vegetable world) is the right kind of friend to hold your hand."

Preheat the oven to 350°F and line a 9in, loose-bottomed pan (preferably with sides 3in deep) with parchment paper and lightly brush the base and sides with a little oil.

Cook the eggplants by puncturing their skins with a skewer, then placing them in a bowl covered with plastic wrap. Microwave on high for 8 minutes, or until the vegetables are cooked and limp. Discard any water at the bottom. Leave the eggplants in the bowl until they are cool enough to handle.

Next, use the tip of a knife to peel the eggplants. Place them in a blender and purée until smooth. Add the chocolate to the eggplant, which will still be warm enough to slowly melt the pieces. Set aside, again covered in plastic wrap, until all the chocolate has melted.

In a bowl, whisk together all the other ingredients for 1 minute until well blended and slightly bubbly. Fold the chocolate and puréed eggplant into the mixture using a spatula and incorporate thoroughly.

Pour the mixture into the prepared pan and place it on the bottom shelf of the oven for 30 minutes, by which time your kitchen will just sing with the smell of hot chocolate.

Remove the cake from the oven and let it cool in its pan for 15 minutes before turning it on to a wire rack and peeling off the parchment. Quickly turn it the right way up again and sit it on a plate to avoid any scars from the rack.

Dust a little cocoa powder over the top of the cake before cutting yourself a slice.

Tips
~ Make sure the eggplant has definitely melted the chocolate. If the eggplant is too cool, simply microwave for another 2 minutes before adding the chocolate chunks.

~ Be very careful to unmold the cake when it is cool rather than warm—it is terribly delicate. A little time to cool down helps make it more robust.

DARK CHOCOLATE, BRANDY, AND CHERRY CAKE

Serves 8

1oz dried cherries
⅓ cup brandy
7oz dark chocolate
  with cherry
8 tablespoons (1 stick)
  unsalted butter
¾ cup superfine sugar
3 large free-range
  eggs, separated
½ cup all-purpose flour
½ cup ground almonds
⅓ cup whole milk
½ teaspoon salt

For the ganache icing
⅓ cup heavy cream
3oz dark (70% cocoa
  solids) chocolate,
  broken into pieces
Crème fraîche, to serve

A huge fan of our dark chocolate and cherry bar, Paul Gayler, the Executive Chef at the Lanesborough Hotel in London, developed this delicious chocolate cake for us.

Soak the dried cherries in the brandy overnight.

The following day, preheat the oven to 375°F. Lightly grease an 8in round cake pan and line with parchment paper.

Melt the chocolate in a microwave or heatproof bowl over a pan of barely simmering water, making sure the bowl doesn't touch the water, stirring from time to time. When almost melted, remove from the heat and continue stirring to melt any remaining lumps. Set aside to cool.

Place the butter and sugar in a bowl and cream together until light and pale in color.

Add the egg yolks one at a time, beating well each time to ensure the mixture is smooth and creamy.

Stir in the cooled melted chocolate, then fold in the flour and ground almonds, the milk, and brandy-soaked cherries. Add the salt.

Whisk the egg whites in a bowl until stiff, and then gently fold into the chocolate mix.

Pour the mixture into the prepared cake pan, level off the surface, and then place in the oven to bake for 45 to 50 minutes.

Leave to cool in the pan for 10 minutes before turning the cake onto a wire rack.

To make the icing, gently heat the chocolate and cream together in a pan then allow to cool and thicken. Spread over the cake to coat.

Cut the warm cake into wedges and top with streaks of the crème fraîche.

Tips

~ Instead of the ganache icing, you could cover the cake with your favorite buttercream to transform it into a decadent birthday cake.

~ You can use whisky if you don't have any brandy in your cupboard.

LINDSEY BAREHAM'S' CHOCOLATE, ALMOND, AND RASPBERRY BIRTHDAY CAKE

Serves 12

For the almond chocolate cake

14 tablespoons unsalted butter, chopped, plus extra for greasing
7oz dark (70% cocoa solids) chocolate, broken into pieces
Pinch of salt
4 large free-range eggs
½ cup superfine sugar
I cup self-rising flour
⅔ cup ground almonds

For the filling

3 tablespoons unsalted butter, chopped
3½oz dark (70% cocoa solids) chocolate, broken into pieces
⅓ cup whipping cream
10½oz firm raspberries

For the marzipan

Apricot jelly
Confectioners' sugar
18oz rolled marzipan
Edible rice paper

For the icing

About 3 tablespoons lemon juice
2½ cups confectioners' sugar, sifted
Silver balls, strips of angelica, and crystallised rose petals, to decorate

You will need parchment paper and a 12in square cake board

I've been making numerical birthday cakes for my grown-up sons since they were toddlers. I don't use special baking numbers, relying on my ingenuity to slice up regular cakes and jelly rolls, then pressing the pieces together, holding everything firm with a marzipan covering. The pieces look an unpromising mess as the cake is carved up but the marzipan covers a multitude of sins and the end result always looks stunning!

Occasionally I make birthday and celebration cakes for friends and this one needed to be pretty and feminine and very chocolatey. I've used the numbers 6 and 0, but the recipe can be adapted for other numbers, and if you don't want to bother with a numerical cake, simply fill and cover the top of the cake with chocolate icing and raspberries.

Preheat the oven to 300°F. Smear the base of an 8in non-stick springform cake pan with butter and line with parchment paper.

Melt the remaining butter and chocolate in a heatproof bowl over a pan of barely simmering water, making sure the bowl doesn't touch the water. Add a pinch of salt and stir occasionally. When smooth and amalgamated, remove the bowl from the heat and leave to cool.

Beat the eggs and sugar for several minutes until pale and fluffy. Beat in the cooled chocolate mixture—it will deflate the mixture slightly—then gradually fold in the flour and almonds. Pour the thick, creamy mixture into the prepared cake pan. Bake for 45 to 50 minutes until firm and risen and a skewer inserted in the center comes out clean. Leave in the pan for 10 minutes before turning on to a wire rack.

To make the chocolate filling, melt the butter and chocolate as before and remove from the heat. Lightly whip the cream and stir into the chocolate butter; it will immediately thicken. Set aside.

As soon as the cake is cooled, slice it in half horizontally and place it back together. Place a 5in saucer at the edge of one side of the cake and cut out a circle. This is going to be the zero. Cut out a 1½in central circle. If you want to increase the size of the zero, cut it in half and use trimmings to plug the gap. Use the remaining cake to fashion the six; I followed the curve of the cake to make the curve of the six and leftovers to make the circle. Don't worry if it looks like a terrible mess; this is a very forgiving recipe. Mix 2 tablespoons boiling water into 4 tablespoons jelly. Dust a work surface, your hands, and a rolling pin with confectioners' sugar and roll out about a quarter of the marzipan very thinly to three to four times its original size. Use a pastry brush to paint the marzipan with the loosened apricot jelly. Place the zero on the marzipan, spread the cut surfaces with chocolate paste, top the base with raspberries, and carefully fit the lid. Entirely cover the zero with jelly-smeared marzipan, cutting and pasting as neatly as you can. Carefully lift onto lightly moistened rice paper (to make it stick). Repeat with the six. Carefully transfer to the cake board. Once the final positions are decided, moisten the rice paper so it sticks to the board to keep the cakes secure.

To make the icing, mix the lemon juice into the sifted confectioners' sugar to make a simple sugar icing. Use an offset spatula to smear it all over the assembled cake. Decorate the cake immediately before the icing sets. I chuck handfuls of silver balls at the cake and make flowers with crystallized rose petals and strips of angelica. Leave the cake in a cool place, not the fridge, for the icing to dry.

CLAUDIA RODEN'S GATEAU AU CHOCOLAT

Flour or matzo meal,
  for dusting
9oz dark (70% cocoa
  solids) chocolate
7 tablespoons unsalted butter
  (optional), plus extra
  for greasing
6 extra-large free-range
  eggs, separated
⅓ cup superfine sugar
⅔ cup ground almonds

Serves 10 to 12

"I featured this chocolate cake in my first Middle Eastern book, and it has since gone into other people's books, so by now it has already had much exposure, but it is still our family favorite and an important recipe in the Passover cake collection. It was given to me by my mother's friend, Lucie Ades-Schwartz. Years later she told me she forgot to put butter in the ingredients list. Although we have come to prefer the butterless cake, I will give her original, richer version and you can please yourself about adding it."

Preheat the oven to 350°F and grease a 10in non-stick cake pan then dust it with flour or matzo meal.

Melt the chocolate and butter in a heatproof bowl over a pan of barely simmering water, making sure the bowl doesn't touch the water, then set aside to cool.

Beat the egg yolks with the sugar until light and fluffy. Add the ground almonds and the melted chocolate and butter and mix thoroughly.

In a separate large bowl, whip the egg whites until stiff and fold them in to the mixture. Pour the mixture into the prepared pan and bake for 30 to 45 minutes or until a skewer inserted in the center of the cake comes out clean.

Tip
~ Decorate with orange zest for a hint of color.

CHOCOLATE AND CHESTNUT SOUFFLÉ CAKE

2 tablespooons soft unsalted butter
9 tablespoons unsalted butter, chopped
4½oz dark (70% cocoa solids) chocolate, broken into pieces
Pinch of salt
9oz can Clément Faugier vanilla chestnut spread
(or 7oz unsweetened chestnut purée mixed with 2 tablespoons superfine sugar)
⅓ cup 1% milk
3 extra-large free-range eggs
⅓ cup superfine sugar
Cocoa powder, for dusting
Crème fraîche, to serve

Serves 8

Dark chocolate and chestnut purée is a subtle marriage made in heaven, particularly in a soufflé cake, says Lindsey Bareham, the creator of this cake. The texture is pure angel food, like soft, luscious mousse-meets-truffle, and incredibly rich, so a small slice is all that even the most dedicated chocoholic will be able to manage. It looks stunning dusted with cocoa and is eaten cold with a scoop of tangy crème fraîche, the lemony zing offering the perfect counter-balance to the rich, dark mousse.

Preheat the oven to 325°F. Smear an 8in flan pan with a removable bottom with half the soft butter. Line the pan with a large sheet of parchment paper, pressing it against the buttery sides, tucking and folding to make the sides smooth and trimming to leave a 2in collar above the rim of the pan. Smear the sides of the parchment as best you can with the remaining soft butter. Place the pan on a baking sheet.

Melt the chopped butter and chocolate in a heatproof bowl over a pan of barely simmering water, making sure the bowl doesn't touch the water. Add a pinch of salt and stir occasionally. When smooth and amalgamated, remove the bowl from the heat and leave to cool.

Heat the chestnut purée with the milk in a small pan, stirring until smooth. Separate the eggs and beat the yolks with the sugar until pale and smooth. Stir the chestnut milk into the cooled chocolate mixture and then into the egg and sugar, stirring to make a smooth batter. Whisk the egg whites until very stiff. Using a metal spoon, quickly stir 1 tablespoon of egg white into the mixture to slacken, then gently fold in the rest. Pour into the prepared flan pan and bake for about 25 minutes, until the cake is puffed and probably cracked but with a slight wobble in the middle. Once out of the oven, the cake will deflate slightly and cracks may begin to appear. Don't worry about this—they add to its charm.

Leave the soufflé to become cold, when it will set further, before removing the collar. Carefully peel the parchment paper off the sides of the cake and trim so the base paper isn't visible. Cover with plastic wrap and chill for at least 2 hours.

Dust with sieved cocoa before serving with crème fraîche (don't forget the base paper when you serve the slices).

ULTIMATE CHOCOLATE FUDGE CAKE

Serves 16

3½oz dark (70% cocoa solids) chocolate, broken into pieces
1⅓ cups all-purpose flour
¾ cup cocoa powder
1 teaspoon baking powder
1 teaspoon baking soda
Pinch of salt
⅔ cup ground almonds
14 tablespoons unsalted butter, softened, plus extra for greasing
1¼ cups light brown sugar
1 teaspoon vanilla extract
3 extra-large free-range eggs, lightly beaten
½ cup buttermilk

For the icing
7oz dark (70% cocoa solids) chocolate, broken into pieces
7oz milk chocolate, broken into pieces
18 tablespoons unsalted butter, softened
Confectioners' sugar, for dusting (optional)

Natalie Seldon runs a gorgeous miniature cake company, but here used one of her own special chocolate recipes to create what can only be described as the "Ultimate" chocolate fudge cake! Deliciously addictive and chocolatey, yet a triumph with it's beautifully light texture, it is comprised of four layers with a glossy elegant chocolate icing—truly making a beautiful centerpiece and treat for any special occasion.

Preheat the oven to 350°F. Grease two 8in pans with sides about 1½in deep and line each with parchment paper.

Melt the chocolate in a heatproof bowl over a pan of barely simmering water, making sure the bowl doesn't touch the water, then set aside to cool.

In a large bowl, sift the flour, cocoa, baking powder, baking soda, and a pinch of salt, then stir in the ground almonds. Using an electric stand or hand-held mixer, cream together the butter and sugar until very light and fluffy. Add the vanilla extract to the eggs. With the beaters running, very slowly add the egg mixture to the butter and sugar, adding 1 tablespoon of the flour mixture during the process to prevent curdling, then add the melted chocolate and buttermilk.

Very gently fold in the remaining flour and divide the mixture between the pans.

Bake on the center shelf for 30 to 35 minutes, or until risen and firm to the touch. Leave the cakes to cool slightly in the pan before turning on to cooling racks.

Once cold, remove the papers and slice each cake in half horizontally through the middle.

To make the icing, melt the chocolate following the method above. Set aside to cool slightly, then beat together with the butter. Using an offset spatula, spread evenly to sandwich the layers together and cover the top of the cake

Decorate with a dusting of confectioners' sugar if you wish.

TORTES, TARTS, PUDDINGS, AND PIES

NICK MALGIERI'S CHOCOLATE BOURBON CAKE

Serves 8 to 10

8 tablespoons (1 stick) unsalted butter, cut into 12 pieces, plus extra for greasing
5½oz dark (70% cocoa solids) chocolate, chopped into ¼in pieces
¼ cup granulated sugar
4 tablespoons all-purpose flour
Pinch of salt
3 large free-range eggs
1½ tablespoons best-quality bourbon
¼ cup dark brown sugar
Whipped cream, to serve

The sweet, mellow flavor of bourbon has a great affinity for chocolate. Serve this unadorned cake with a little unsweetened whipped cream.

Position a rack in the top third of the oven and preheat it to 350°F. Thoroughly butter an 8in round, 2in deep pan.

Melt the butter in a saucepan over medium heat, allowing it to sizzle and get really hot. Remove from the heat, add the chocolate, and whisk until smooth.

Whisk the granulated sugar, flour, and salt together, then add all the eggs and the bourbon. Whisk together smoothly.

Stir the brown sugar into the cooled chocolate mixture and stir into the batter. Pour the batter into the prepared pan and smooth the top. Bake the cake for 25 minutes.

Stand the pan on a wire rack, then cool the cake in the pan. Unmold the cake onto a serving plate and serve in slices with whipped cream.

VELVET SALTED CARAMEL CHOCOLATE TORTE

Serves 12

For the salted caramel

¾ cup golden superfine sugar

3 tablespoons water

½ cup heavy cream

½ teaspoon sea salt flakes

9 tablespoons unsalted butter, cubed

For the torte

9oz dark (70-85% cocoa solids) chocolate, broken into pieces

11 tablespoons unsalted butter, cubed

¾ cup golden baker's sugar

1 teaspoon vanilla extract

¾ cup ground almonds

5 large free-range egg yolks

6 extra-large free-range egg whites

Cream or good vanilla ice cream, to serve

Alice Hart, who contributed this recipe, feels "there must be something in the alchemy of salt, deep caramel, and darkest chocolate. Something highly addictive I'd bet, for it keeps me dreaming up new ways to marry the three. This fallen soufflé cake, with a texture like velvet, has a ribbon of amber caramel and the merest hint of salt flowing through it. It is a truly divine dessert but is terribly rich so do serve it in fine slices with chilled cream or ice cream to cut through the sweetness. And of course, there's no flour in the recipe, making it suitable for those with wheat allergies."

Start a good few hours before you want to eat the cake, beginning by making the salted caramel. Pour the sugar into a heavy-bottomed pan and add the water. Heat gently, stirring only until the sugar dissolves. Turn the heat up to medium-high and allow the syrup to come to a boil undisturbed. Simmer briskly and watch like a hawk until the caramel turns a rich amber color. Swirl the pan to prevent "hot spots" but don't stir (stirring causes the caramel to clump and crystallize). Remove the pan from the heat and carefully stir in the cream and salt: there's sure to be a hiss and a good splatter. Now stir in the butter cubes until a smooth caramel forms and set aside to cool.

Preheat the oven to 350°F. Line a 9in springform cake pan with parchment paper.

Melt the chocolate, butter, and sugar together in a heatproof bowl set over a pan of barely simmering water, making sure the bowl doesn't touch the water (or you can melt everything in a saucepan set over very low heat, but don't allow it to burn). Remove from the heat and stir until smooth, then mix in the vanilla and almonds, followed by the egg yolks, one by one.

Whisk the egg whites in a clean bowl until they form stiff peaks. Fold 1 large tablespoon into the chocolate mixture with a metal spoon or a spatula to loosen it, then fold in the rest, being careful to retain as much air as possible. Scrape about two-thirds of this batter into the pan. Make a slight dip in the center and spoon the salted caramel into the dip and over the surface. Top with the remaining chocolate mixture, smoothing it right to the edges. Bake for about 40 minutes, until puffed and barely firm. There might be some caramel bubbling up at the edges but that's absolutely fine—resist the temptation to touch it because it will be scalding hot.

Leave to cool completely in the pan; the cake will gently crumple in the center. Slice and serve each velvety piece at room temperature with chilled whipped cream, or some really good vanilla ice cream.

"OLD ENGLISH" CHOCOLATE FLAN

For the dough
1 cup ground almonds
¼ cup superfine sugar
1 extra-large free-range
  egg white
Flour, for dusting

For the filling
8oz dark (70% or
  85% cocoa solids)
  chocolate, broken
  into pieces
1 cup half-and-half
Whipped cream, to serve

Serves 8

I've seen this recipe in a few books and I like it because it is incredibly simple, using only a few ingredients, and the texture changes over time. Eat it when just set and it has a crisp shell and a soft filling. Leave it overnight and the shell softens and the filling stiffens, giving a fudgier flan.

Blend the almonds and sugar together, then mix to a smooth paste with the egg white.

Tightly wrap the dough in plastic wrap and let it rest in the fridge for at least 1 hour.

Preheat the oven to 350°F and line a 9in flan or springform pan with parchment paper.

Roll out the dough on a lightly floured work surface. It will be very brittle but do try to roll it fairly thinly. The dough will also tend to stick to the rolling pin. You can prevent this from happening by dusting your rolling pin with flour.

Line the pan with the pastry, allowing a 1½in rim: you may well need to do a bit of patchwork here. Bake in the center of the oven for 30 minutes until the pastry is light golden brown. Check halfway through cooking that it is cooking evenly; if not, give it a turn. Remove from the oven and set aside to cool.

Meanwhile, melt the chocolate in a microwave or heatproof bowl over a pan of barely simmering water, making sure the bowl doesn't touch the water, then set aside to cool.

Add the cream to the chocolate and mix thoroughly. Pour this mixture into the cooled pastry case, and leave to set at room temperature for 1 hour.

Serve with a little whipped cream.

CHOCOLATE TART

Serves 6

For the shortcrust pastry

1 cup plus 2 tablespoons
  all-purpose flour
¼ cup confectioners' sugar
5 tablespoons unsalted butter,
  chilled and cut into small
  cubes
1 extra-large free-range
  egg yolk

For the tart mix

½ cup plus 1 tablespoon
  heavy cream
¼ cup 1% milk
6oz dark (70% cocoa solids)
  chocolate, broken into pieces
1 extra-large free-range egg,
  plus 1 extra-large free-range
  egg yolk, beaten

This is Tom Aikens' perfect chocolate tart mix. We've used our favorite sweet pastry tart shell but, if you are in a rush, Tom recommends using good-quality store-bought pastry. The chocolate mixture is very versatile and can be used in any number of desserts. Try combining with sponge cake and whipped cream for a makeshift trifle or with whipped cream, crushed meringue, and your chosen fruit for a twist on an Eton Mess.

For the pastry, sift the flour and confectioners' sugar. In a food processor, mix together the flour, sugar, and butter until you have a texture similar to breadcrumbs. Add the egg yolk and mix together until the ingredients more or less come together. It's important not to over mix. If the pastry looks a bit dry or crumbly, add a tiny splash of milk or water. Shape into a disc, wrap in plastic wrap, and refrigerate for a minimum of 1 hour.

Grate the pastry on a coarse grater and press it evenly around the edges and base of the tart pan to a thickness of 1 to 2 inches. Prick the base with a fork and leave to rest in the fridge for 30 minutes.

Preheat the oven to 350°F. To prevent the pastry from shrinking too much or sinking down, put a disc of parchment paper inside the tart shell before baking and fill it with rice or lentils. The parchment paper must be bigger than the tart shell to keep rice or lentils from getting stuck in the pastry. Start baking the tart shell on the top shelf of the oven, then after 10 minutes take the tart shell out and if the pastry looks like it has "dried out" all over, remove the parchment paper and rice/lentils. Continue cooking for 5 to 10 minutes until light brown. Remove and cool on a rack.

Turn down the oven to 225°F.

Place the cream, milk, and chocolate in a saucepan over low heat, stirring from time to time, until the chocolate has melted. Remove the pan from the heat and whisk in the egg and egg yolk.

Pour the mixture into the tart case and bake for 45 minutes.

PEAR AND CHOCOLATE TATIN

Serves 8 to 10

For the pastry
(or use one package of
prepared, all-butter
puff pastry)
1 cup all-purpose flour
⅛ cup cocoa powder
¼ teaspoon salt
7 tablespoons cold butter
1½ tablespoons superfine
sugar
2 extra-large free-range
egg yolks

For the filling
4 to 5 Bosc pears
4 tablespoons (½ stick)
unsalted butter
¼ cup raw sugar
2oz dark (70% cocoa
solids) chocolate, grated
Vanilla ice cream, to serve

Pears and chocolate have a great affinity. G&B's fan, Harriet Hewitson, brings them together well here in a traditional tatin; after caramelizing the pears but before laying over the pastry and baking, she cleverly but simply grates some chocolate over the pears which melts into both the fruit and the pastry. Using only half a bar ensures this tart is not too heavy and the chocolate doesn't dominate.

Preheat the oven to 375°F.

To make the pastry, process the flour, cocoa, salt, and butter until they resemble breadcrumbs. Add the superfine sugar then gently mix in the 2 egg yolks. Knead the pastry together and then chill for 30 minutes in the fridge.

For the filling, peel and core the pears and cut into quarters. Melt the butter in a 10in ovenproof frying pan or a tarte tatin dish, then add the raw sugar and allow the two to turn syrupy and begin to caramelize. Carefully arrange the pears in a wheel around the center, round side down, and allow to caramelize for 5 to 10 minutes. While the fruit is cooking, sprinkle with the grated chocolate. Allow the dish to cool.

Roll out the pastry and cut it to fit the dish, then gently lower the pastry onto the fruit. Carefully make a few holes in the pastry. Place in the oven and cook for 20 to 25 minutes until the pastry is brown and crispy.

Very carefully invert the tarte onto a dish and serve with ice cream.

LORRAINE PASCALE'S CHOCOLATE BANOFFEE TART

Serves 8 to 10

For the toffee layer
1 (14oz) can of
 condensed milk

For the chocolate pastry
2 extra-large free-range
 egg yolks
Seeds from 1 vanilla bean
 or 2 drops of vanilla
 extract
½ cup sugar
7 tablespoons unsalted butter,
 softened
1⅓ cups all-purpose flour
⅓ cup cocoa powder
Pinch of salt

For the banana layer
2 tablespoons unsalted butter
3 bananas, sliced
3 tablespoons rum
Seeds from ½ vanilla bean
 or 2 drops of vanilla
 extract

For the cream top
½ cup heavy whipping cream
1¾ tablespoons confectioners'
 sugar
Seeds of ½ vanilla bean
 or 2 drops of vanilla
 extract

To decorate
1½oz dark (70% cocoa solids)
 chocolate and 1½oz white
 chocolate, grated

Move over banana cream pie, there's a new dessert in town. A rich chocolate tart with rum-laced bananas and layers of toffee and cream. Deliciously naughty.

Begin by placing the unopened can of condensed milk in a medium pan. Cover it with water and boil for 2 hours. Top off the water level as needed.

To make the pastry, mix together the yolks, vanilla, and sugar. Add the butter and mix briefly until well combined. Add the flour, cocoa powder, and salt. Once the flour is added, use as few strokes as possible to bring the mixture together. This way the pastry will remain crumbly and tender when cooked.

Scoop up the pastry with your hand and bring together to form a ball. Wrap it in plastic wrap and place in the fridge for 30 minutes. Preheat the oven to 400°F.

Remove the pastry from the fridge and roll it out to the thickness of a quarter. Place a 10in flan ring on a baking sheet and line it with the pastry. Take a small ball of pastry rolled in flour (about the size of a hazelnut) and use it to ease the pastry into the "corners" of the flan ring. Using a sharp knife, cut off the excess of the pastry around the top of the ring. Then run a small sharp knife around the edge between the pastry and the flan ring to loosen slightly. This makes it much easier to demold once it is cooked.

Place the lined flan ring in the fridge for 10 minutes.

Cut a large circle of parchment paper slightly larger than the flan ring. Scrunch it up and then unscrunch it and place it in the flan ring. Fill the pastry with pie weights or dried beans and bake in

the oven for 20 minutes or until it feels firm to the touch. Remove the paper and weights and return it to the oven for another 10 minutes to cook the base. The chocolate content means the pastry will burn easily so if you see the edges getting dark, cover them with foil to prevent further browning. The base of the pastry is ready when it feels sandy to the touch and firm. Put the tart in the fridge to set.

When the pastry is cooked, remove it from the oven and set aside to cool for 5 minutes, before removing it from the pan. Don't leave it for too long in the pan as it can be impossible to remove it!

For the banana layer, melt the butter in a medium pan, then add the bananas, rum, and vanilla. Cook until the bananas have softened slightly and set aside.

Whip the cream, confectioners' sugar, and vanilla until it holds its shape and set aside.

To assemble, remove the condensed milk from the pan, spoon it into the tart, and then layer the bananas over the top. Cover the surface completely with the whipped cream and sprinkle the grated chocolate before serving.

PURE GOLD SEA SALTED CHOCOLATE GINGER TART WITH FENNEL SEED BRITTLE

Serves 8 generous
 portions or 4 super
 indulgent portions

For the crust
6 tablespoons unsalted butter
3 tablespoons light muscovado
 sugar
I extra-large free-range
 egg yolk
I cup all-purpose flour
½ teaspoon sea salt—
 choose your favorite
 brand

For the filling
3½oz Maya Gold chocolate
3½oz dark chocolate
 with ginger
⅔ cup heavy cream
½ cup light muscovado
 sugar
I teaspoon sea salt
I teaspoon malt extract
 (available in large
 supermarkets)

For the brittle crust
½ cup golden baker's or
 granulated sugar
½oz fennel seeds

Paul Young is famous for blending unusual and unexpected ingredients into chocolate, but he also loves the classics just approached from a new angle: "Creating new flavor combinations, textures, and styles is my true passion so I am thrilled to be sharing this recipe with you using my two favorite Green & Black's chocolate bars and some of my dearly loved ingredients—sea salt and fennel seeds.

"My philosophy is 'Taste one new thing every day, something you wouldn't usually choose,' and wait. It's amazing what you can discover, and this new recipe was inspired this way by munching through all the wonderful Green & Black's bars, some of which I had never tried. I chose Maya gold with its warming spices and the intense 60% cocoa solids ginger bar and muddled them both into this stunning tart ideal for a dinner party dessert, afternoon tea, or a special indulgent mid-week treat. It's surprisingly easy to make too.

p.s Fennel seeds and chocolate make a jaw dropping combination with crunch and delicate anise flavors but feel free to replace them with your favorite seed such as poppy, pumpkin, sunflower, or sesame."

To make the crust, cream together the butter and sugar with a wooden spoon until creamy and pale in color. Add the yolks and 1 tablespoon cold water and mix until incorporated. Mix the salt into the flour, then gradually add the flour mix, stirring well until a stiff dough is formed. Use a mixer or food processor if this becomes heavy work. Wrap the dough in plastic wrap or foil and refrigerate for 1 hour.

Dust your surface with flour and knead the dough until soft and pliable. Roll out until the dough is 2in bigger than your tart pan (use an 8in loose-bottomed fluted or plain tart pan). Handle with care, but if the dough splits, do not worry as it is easily pressed back together.

Carefully lift the rolled out dough onto the tart pan, pressing into the edges well. Place on a tray and refrigerate for 15 minutes to relax the dough and to prevent shrinkage.

Preheat the oven to 350°F. Line the tart with parchment paper, scrunching it up in your hands to soften it and pour in pie weights, dried peas, lentils, or rice to weigh the paper down. Bake the tart in the oven for 20 minutes, lift out the parchment and pie weights, and re-bake for 5 minutes until golden. (Now the tricky part is over!)

To make the filling, place all the ingredients in a mixing bowl and place over a pan of gently simmering water but NOT boiling as this will overcook the filling. Mix well.

Once smooth and glossy, pour into the tart base and refrigerate for 2 hours.

Remove from the fridge and, using a very sharp knife, trim off any excess pastry from the tart edges and discard. Place the tart onto a presentation plate ready for serving.

To finish, make the brittle by slowly warming the sugar in a large saucepan over medium heat until it begins to dissolve and become golden. Stir carefully with a wooden spoon until all lumps are gone, then pour in the seeds, mixing well. Immediately pour the sugar and seed mixture onto a baking sheet lined with parchment and allow to become fully cold.

Once cold, smash it up until it looks like glass shards and scatter across the tart.

Serve with pride and a generous scoop of real vanilla bean ice cream.

Tips
~ Make the pastry beforehand and freeze or refrigerate for up to 3 days until needed. Or, you can even line your tart pan in plastic wrap and foil, freeze until needed, then bake.

~You can also create your own delicious combination by choosing your own two favorite Green and Black's chocolate bars.

DARINA ALLEN'S CHOCOLATE AND PEANUT BUTTER PIE

Serves 8

7 tablespoons unsalted butter

3½oz dark (70% cocoa solids) chocolate, chopped

2 tablespoons strong coffee (preferably espresso)

1 (10in) ready-made sweet shortcrust pastry case

¼ cup full-fat cream cheese

⅓ cup confectioners' sugar

⅓ cup smooth peanut butter

2 tablespoons 1% milk

5 tablespoons heavy cream

Confectioners' sugar, for dusting

This pie has an all-American flavor and the wow factor for a dinner party dessert.

Melt the butter and chocolate together in a heatproof bowl over a pan of barely simmering water, making sure the bowl doesn't touch the water. Whisk in the coffee and leave it to set slightly. Pour into the pastry and refrigerate while you make the rest of the filling.

Put the cream cheese, confectioners' sugar, peanut butter, and milk into a food processor and process for a few seconds or until smooth.

Whip the cream until soft peaks form. Transfer the peanut butter mixture into a mixing bowl and fold the cream into the mixture. Pour into the pastry, smooth the top, and leave to set completely in a cool place; this takes about 4 to 5 hours.

Dust the tart with confectioners' sugar just before serving.

CHOCOLATE PUDDING PIE

Serves 10 to 12

For the base

6 tablespoons butter, plus
   extra for greasing
2½oz dark (70 to 85%
   cocoa solids) chocolate
8oz Graham crackers

For the filling

13 tablespoons unsalted butter
6oz dark (70% cocoa solids)
   chocolate, broken
   into pieces
4 large free-range eggs
¾ cup dark muscovado
   sugar
⅔ cup heavy cream
Crème fraîche, to serve

Millie Charters is famous among her friends for her baking! Her recent maternity leave has been put to good use developing various recipes, including this delicious Chocolate Pudding Pie that she sent in to us. A favorite on the photo shoot, it looks stunning topped with summer berries and a light dusting of confectioners' sugar.

Preheat the oven to 350°F.

For the base, melt the butter and chocolate in a heatproof bowl over a pan of barely simmering water, making sure the bowl doesn't touch the water. Stir until completely melted and combined. Crush the Graham crackers (I use a blender) into fine crumbs and add to the melted mixture.

Butter the base and sides of a 9in loose-bottomed pan. Put the base in the pan, press it down, and let it chill for half an hour in the fridge.

Meanwhile, melt the butter and dark chocolate for the filling in the same way. Put the eggs, sugar, and cream in the blender and mix together. Allow the melted chocolate mixture to cool (otherwise you risk the cream curdling). Once cool, add the melted chocolate mixture to the blender and blend together again, making sure that all the sugar is mixed in.

Remove the base from the fridge and pour the filling over the top. Put in the oven and cook for 45 minutes until firm. It will rise up as it cooks but, once removed, will shrink again slightly.

Allow to cool and serve with a generous serving of crème fraîche.

Tip
~ *This is delicious made the day before and means you can avoid last-minute panics.*

CHOCOLATE MERINGUE PIE

Serves 6 to 8

For the pastry
1 cup plus 2 tablespoons
   all-purpose flour
¼ cup confectioners' sugar
5 tablespoons chilled unsalted
   butter, cut into small cubes
1 extra-large free-range
   egg yolk

For the custard
4 extra-large egg yolks
¼ cup superfine sugar
2 tablespoons all-purpose flour
1 cup plus 3 tablespoons
   whole milk
3oz dark (70% cocoa solids)
   chocolate, chopped finely

For the meringue
1½ cups superfine sugar
5 extra-large egg whites

You definitely need electric beaters or an electric mixer to make this meringue, as it is what is known as a hot meringue where you cook the egg whites with hot sugar so it doesn't need to be baked. Also invest in a blowtorch (relatively cheap, surprisingly useful, and, of course, massive fun; a must in the gadget arsenal of a savvy cook).

To make the pastry, begin by sifting the flour and confectioners' sugar together. Rub in the butter to achieve the texture of breadcrumbs. Add the egg yolk and mix until the ingredients come together, using a tiny amount of cold water if needed. Shape into a ball, flatten slightly, wrap in plastic wrap, and chill for at least 1 hour.

Preheat the oven to 425°F. Coarsely grate the pastry into a loose-bottomed 10in tart pan and press it evenly into the edges and base (this is a foolproof way of making a pastry shell). Prick the base and put the pan in the fridge for 30 minutes.

Bake the tart shell for 10 to 15 minutes. Remove and cool on a wire rack.

Meanwhile, make the custard. Whisk together the egg yolks and sugar, then sift in the flour and whisk that in. Heat the milk to a boil, then pour onto the egg mixture, whisking constantly. Return the mixture to the saucepan and bring to a boil over low heat, still whisking. When it comes to a boil, continue to whisk constantly for another 5 minutes, still over low heat. It will be thick and smooth. Remove from the heat and add the chocolate, whisking until fully melted and incorporated. Pour into a bowl, cover the surface with plastic wrap to prevent a skin from forming, and leave to cool.

To make the meringue, reduce the oven temperature to 400°F. Pour the sugar onto a baking sheet and place in the oven for 7 minutes. Meanwhile, beat the egg whites until stiff using electric beaters or an electric mixer. Remove the sugar from the oven and quickly decant into a heatproof container. Set the beaters/mixer on the lowest setting and slowly pour the sugar (taking a couple of minutes) on to the egg whites.

To assemble, put the chocolate custard into the cooled pastry and spread to form an even layer. Pour or spoon the meringue over the custard, beginning in the center to allow it to slightly flow to the edges. I like the natural bumps and mounds, but it can be smoothed with an offset spatula. Fire up a blowtorch and color the meringue all over.

Serve to squeals of delight.

CHOCOLATE AND PECAN PIE

Serves 8

All-purpose flour, for dusting

9oz ready-made sweet
   shortcrust pastry

3oz dark (70% cocoa solids)
   chocolate, finely chopped

5 tablespoons unsalted butter

2 large free-range eggs

⅓ cup superfine sugar

½ cup corn syrup

1 teaspoon vanilla
   extract

3½oz pecans, finely
   chopped, plus 3½oz
   pecan halves, to decorate

Good Housekeeping readers love Green & Black's. How do we know? Because our chocolate has won many awards in the annual *Good Housekeeping* Food Awards, including probably our favorite award of all time: Favorite Comfort Food, as voted for by the readers. All recipes at *Good Housekeeping* are, famously, triple-tested by the *Good Housekeeping* Institute—and here's the pie that their foodie team put forward as the ultimate recipe, using our 70% dark chocolate.

Preheat the oven to 350°F. Place a baking sheet in the oven to heat up.

Lightly dust the work surface with flour and roll out the shortcrust pastry to the thickness of a quarter. Use it to line an 8in loose-bottomed quiche pan with 1¼in straight-edged sides but do not trim off the excess. Chill until needed.

Melt the chocolate and butter in a heatproof bowl over a pan of barely simmering water, making sure the bowl doesn't touch the water. Cool slightly.

Place the eggs, sugar, corn syrup, vanilla extract, and cooled chocolate mixture in a large bowl and beat together until smooth. Fold in the chopped pecans, then pour into the pastry. Trim the pastry to ½in above the filling. Decorate the surface with the pecan halves.

Transfer the pie to the hot baking sheet in the oven and bake for 40 to 45 minutes until just set.

Serve warm or at room temperature with cream or vanilla ice cream.

ULTIMATE CHOCOLATE FONDANT

Serves 6

4½oz dark (70% cocoa solids) chocolate

9 tablespoons unsalted butter, cut into small pieces, plus extra for greasing

4 extra-large free-range eggs

⅓ cup superfine sugar

⅓ cup plus 1 tablespoon self-rising flour, plus extra for dusting

This chocolate fondant recipe was given to us by James Tanner, who has excelled at the challenge of making a quick and easy dessert that works. For that retro, black forest gâteau taste, serve with vanilla cream and cherries with kirsch.

Melt the chocolate and butter together in a heatproof bowl over a pan of barely simmering water, making sure the bowl doesn't touch the water. Stir until combined then leave to cool.

Preheat the oven to 350°F. Lightly butter and flour six ⅓ cup dariole molds.

Whisk the eggs and sugar together until light and pale and doubled in volume.

Fold the egg mixture into the cooled chocolate. Sift in the flour and, using a large metal spoon, fold until combined.

Spoon the chocolate mixture into the prepared molds and bake for 8 to 9 minutes until risen—the key is to have a runny center. Loosen around each fondant with a knife and carefully turn onto serving plates.

GLUTEN-FREE CHOCOLATE FUDGE PUDDING

Serves 6 to 8

5½oz dark (70% cocoa
    solids) chocolate,
    broken into pieces
11 tablespoons unsalted butter,
    plus extra for greasing
1 teaspoon vanilla extract
½ cup warm water
½ cup superfine sugar
4 large free-range
    eggs, separated
2½ tablespoons rice flour
1 teaspoon gluten-free
    baking powder
Confectioners' sugar,
    for dusting
Softly whipped cream,
    to serve

Your friends will be lining up for invitations to dinner when you serve this delectable pudding, especially when they realize it's gluten free. Darina Allen, who wrote this recipe for all her gluten-free followers, suggests adding some freshly roasted hazelnuts and a dash of Frangelico to the whipped cream for extra pizazz.

Preheat the oven to 400°F. Grease a 1.2-quart pie dish or 6 to 8 ramekins.

Melt the chocolate and butter in a heatproof bowl over a pan of barely simmering water, making sure the bowl doesn't touch the water. As soon as the chocolate has melted, remove from the heat and add the vanilla extract, then stir in the warm water and sugar. Continue to mix until smooth.

Lightly beat the egg yolks and whisk them into the chocolate mixture. Fold in the sifted rice flour and gluten-free baking powder, making sure there are no lumps.

Whisk the egg whites in a large, scrupulously clean bowl until stiff peaks form. Fold gently into the chocolate mixture and pour into the greased pie dish or ramekins.

Put the pie dish into a bain-marie of hot water and bake for 10 minutes (for the single dish), then reduce the temperature to 300°F for another 20 to 30 minutes. If you are using individual dishes, they will be cooked in about 15 minutes at 400°F. The pudding should be firm on the top but still soft and fudgy underneath.

Dust with confectioners' sugar and serve hot, warm, or cold with softly whipped cream.

CHOCOLATE STEAMED PUDDING

Serves 6 to 8

5½oz dark (70% cocoa
  solids) chocolate
9 tablespoons unsalted butter,
  plus extra for greasing
⅔ cup superfine sugar
1⅓ cups all-purpose flour
¼ cup cocoa powder
1 teaspoon baking
  powder
Couple of pinches
  of salt
2 extra-large free-range eggs
2 tablespoons whole milk
Half-and-half, to serve

I am constantly surprised that so many "chocolate" cake, pudding, and ice cream recipes contain cocoa and no chocolate. As a result, they don't taste of chocolate. This is a classic steamed pudding recipe with a generous drizzle of dark chocolate.

Melt the chocolate in a microwave or in a heatproof bowl over a pan of barely simmering water, making sure the bowl doesn't touch the water, then set aside to cool.

Cream the butter and sugar until light and fluffy.

Sift together the flour, cocoa powder, baking powder, and salt.

Beat together the eggs and milk, then mix in the cooled melted chocolate.

Beat the flour mixture and the chocolate mixture alternately into the creamed butter until it is thoroughly blended.

Using a quart pudding basin as a stencil, cut out a circle of parchment paper and smear it with butter.

Pour the mixture into the pudding basin, cover with the parchment paper circle, then cover with a piece of pleated foil (this allows the pudding to rise). Secure the foil by tying a piece of string around the lip of the basin, and fashion a makeshift handle across the top for easy removal.

Bring no more than 2in of water to simmer in a steamer (or you can use a deep saucepan with an upturned saucer in the base) and carefully lower the pudding basin into the pan. Cover and steam for 2 hours. Keep an eye on the water level and add water from a teapot as necessary.

Carefully lift the basin from the steamer, remove the foil and parchment paper, and invert the pudding onto a plate.

Serve with cold half-and-half.

CHOCOLATE AND RASPBERRY CROISSANT PUDDING

Serves 6 to 8

1 tablespoon unsalted butter

3½oz dark (70% cocoa solids) chocolate, chopped into rough chunks, plus 1 tablespoon, finely grated

4 croissants

3½oz frozen raspberries, or fresh in season

2 cups half-and-half

3½oz milk chocolate, chopped

3 large free-range eggs, beaten

Antony Perring is a food stylist and writer in Sydney. He came up with this idea when he had some leftover croissants. You can use fresh raspberries if they are in season.

Preheat the oven to 350°F.

Grease a 2-quart, ovenproof dish with the unsalted butter and dust with grated dark chocolate.

Tear the croissants into chunks and place in the ovenproof dish. Sprinkle the frozen raspberries and chunks of the dark chocolate over the top. Set the dish aside while you prepare the custard mixture.

In a small saucepan, bring the half-and-half up to a boil. Remove from the heat and gently stir in the milk chocolate until melted.

Add the eggs and quickly mix in until well combined. Pour the mixture over the croissants and raspberries. Push the croissants down into the custard so that they soak up a little of the liquid.

Bake in the preheated oven for 20 minutes or until the custard is just set.

Serve hot from the oven with ice cream.

CHOCOLATE STICKY TOFFEE PUDDING CAKE

Serves 6 to 8

For the cake

2 cups boiling water

5½oz chopped dates

5½oz dark (70% cocoa solids) chocolate

7 tablespoons unsalted butter, softened

⅔ cup light brown sugar or light muscovado sugar

3 extra-large free-range eggs

1¾ cups all-purpose flour

1 teaspoon baking soda

1 teaspoon baking powder

For the toffee sauce

¾ cup corn syrup

1¼ cups light brown sugar

7 tablespoons butter

¾ cup cream

½ teaspoon vanilla extract

Sticky toffee pudding is good. Chocolate sticky toffee pudding is even better. Make this with unctuous Medjool dates and you will have a cake so toothsome that the only thing better would be the delightful company of the author of this recipe, the lovely Anita Kinniburgh of Green & Black's (see Anita's Wonderful Whoopie Pies, page 32).

Preheat the oven to 350°F. Grease the sides of an 8in springform pan and line the base with a round disc of parchment paper.

Put the water in a saucepan, reduce to a simmer, and soak the dates in it for 10 minutes. Meanwhile, melt the chocolate in a microwave, or in a heatproof bowl over a pan of barely simmering water, making sure the bowl doesn't touch the water, then set aside to cool.

Cream the softened butter and sugar in a large bowl until light and fluffy. Beat in the eggs, one by one, and then mix in the melted chocolate.

Sift in the flour, baking soda, and baking powder, then add the dates and their soaking liquid and stir to mix. Pour the mixture into the prepared pan and bake in the oven for 50 minutes until it feels springy to touch or a sharp knife inserted into the middle comes out clean.

To make the toffee sauce, place all the ingredients into a saucepan over high heat and boil for 4 to 5 minutes, stirring regularly.

Serve the cake warm on a large plate and pour a generous amount of the hot toffee sauce over the top. Pour the rest into a bowl and pass around for people to help themselves.

CHOCOLATE CHARLOTTE

Serves 6 to 8

14 tablespoons unsalted butter
10 slices medium-sliced white bread (approximately), crusts removed
2 tablespoons demerara sugar
4½oz dark (70% cocoa solids) chocolate, broken into pieces

2 extra-large free-range eggs
¾ cup superfine sugar
½ teaspoon vanilla extract
⅔ cup all-purpose flour
Pinch or two of salt
Heavy cream, to serve

I created this recipe when thinking how I could convert one of my favorite desserts, apple charlotte, into a chocolate version. I decided to fill the bread lining with my favorite brownie recipe and cook it at a slightly lower temperature to ensure that the bread would be caramelized, but not burnt, while the brownie center would set next to the bread, giving a brownie layer, but not in the center which would be molten. A great combination of textures—crisp, soft, liquid— and a big chocolatey hit, with the always pleasing contrast of hot and cold. Oh, and I know what you're thinking: "What's with the white bread?" Trust me. It works.

You need a 1.2-quart pudding basin and a plate to fit on top to keep the dessert weighted down during baking. The cooking time is based on using a china basin. Preheat the oven to 350°F.

Melt the butter in a small pan over low heat. Meanwhile, cut five of the bread slices in half lengthwise.

When the butter has melted, brush the basin and the underside of the plate (to be used as a lid) with the butter. Sprinkle both with the demerara sugar and lightly shake off any excess.

Take four of the remaining slices of bread and arrange into a square. Put the top of the basin over these and cut around the rim to make a circle. Brush butter on one side of these quarter circles and reserve. Take the last whole piece of the bread and trim it to fit in the bottom of the basin. Brush one side with butter and place it butter-side down in the bowl. Brush one side of the half slices of bread with butter and place them butter-side down around the sides of the basin, ensuring that they overlap slightly. They may need trimming slightly to fit the basin; the slices should come to the top of the bowl but not above. Set aside.

Add the chocolate to the remaining butter in the pan, place over low heat, and whisk until melted, being careful not to burn the chocolate. Remove from the heat.

In a bowl, whisk the eggs, sugar, and vanilla extract until thick and creamy. Add a third of the chocolate mix to the egg mix and whisk until combined. Add the remainder and whisk until fully incorporated. Sift the flour and salt together and then add to the chocolate mixture, whisking together until thoroughly mixed in. Pour the mixture into the basin, using a spatula to ensure none is wasted. Place the reserved bread circle, butter-side up, over the chocolate mixture. Place the buttered and sugared plate on top of the bread lid and press down firmly but slowly until the plate's rim touches the top of the basin's rim. Place on a baking sheet and bake for 1 hour.

Remove the plate and replace with a larger plate and invert the plate and basin together, being careful not to burn your hands. Now lift off the inverted bowl revealing the crisp, caramelized bread.

Allow to rest for a few minutes, then use a sharp knife to cut through the bread crust to reveal a layer of rich cake and a molten chocolate center. Serve with cold cream.

RETRO CHERRY CHOCOLATE AND ALMOND JELLY ROLL

Serves 8

For the crunchy almonds
2 teaspoons corn syrup
¼ cup superfine sugar
2 tablespoons water
Pinch of salt (optional)
1½ cups slivered almonds

7oz dark (70% cocoa
  solids) chocolate,
  broken into pieces
¾ cup superfine sugar
6 extra-large free-range
  eggs, separated
2 level tablespoons
  cocoa powder, sifted

For the filling
Cherry Chocolate Mousse
  (see opposite)

**For the Cherry Chocolate
  Mousse**
7oz dark chocolate with
  cherry, broken into pieces
1 teaspoon unsalted butter
4 extra-large free-range
  eggs, separated
2 tablespoons kirsch/cherry
  brandy (optional)

To serve
Confectioners' sugar, to dust
Fresh or canned cherries,
  depending on season
Crème fraîche or whipped
  cream

This sensational adaption of the retro jelly roll was given to us by Maria Elia. You can serve the chocolate cherry mousse on its own when you're in a hurry and you will still impress your guests.

Preheat the oven to 350°F. Lightly grease a 13 x 9in jelly roll pan and line with parchment paper.

First make the crunchy almonds. Bring the corn syrup, sugar, and water to a boil in a small pan. If you like your caramel with a salty edge, add a pinch of salt. Add in the almonds and stir until coated. Drain the excess caramel off the nuts using a slotted spoon.

Spread the almonds on a baking sheet in a single layer. Bake for about 8 minutes until golden brown.

Allow to cool to room temperature.

Melt the chocolate in a heatproof bowl over a pan of barely simmering water, making sure the bowl doesn't touch the water. Stir until completely melted then set aside to cool slightly.

Place the sugar and egg yolks in a bowl and whisk until light and creamy. Add the cooled chocolate and stir until evenly blended.

Whisk the egg whites until stiff peaks form. Using a metal spoon, fold in a large spoonful of the egg whites into the chocolate mixture, mix gently, and then fold in the remaining egg whites, followed by the cocoa powder. Pour into the prepared pan and gently level the surface.

Bake for about 18 to 20 minutes until firm to the touch, then remove the roulade from the oven, leave in the pan, and place a cooling rack over the top of the cake. Leave to cool.

Dust a large piece of parchment paper with confectioners' sugar. Turn the roulade onto the paper and peel off the lining paper.

Spread with the cherry chocolate mousse and scatter with the almonds; roll up jelly-roll style, starting from one of the short edges—use the paper to help you. It will crack, but don't worry, it adds to its charm!

Serve with the cherries and a generous serving of crème fraîche.

For the Cherry Chocolate Mousse

Melt the chocolate and butter in a heatproof bowl over a pan of barely simmering water, making sure the bowl doesn't touch the water. Stir until completely melted and combined, then remove the bowl from the pan and allow to cool slightly.

Place the egg whites in a large clean, dry bowl and whisk until stiff peaks form.

Beat the egg yolks and kirsch, if using, into the cooled chocolate.

Using a large metal spoon, fold in the egg whites until completely combined.

Chill in the fridge for at least 2 hours.

Tip
~ *Try using different flavors of chocolate: cherry, ginger, white chocolate, espresso, or butterscotch.*

GINGER AND DARK CHOCOLATE ROULADE WITH POACHED PEARS

For the pears
2 large pears, peeled, cored, and each sliced into 16 crescents
1 vanilla bean, split in half
2 heaping tablespoons superfine sugar
1¾ cups water

For the roulade
7oz dark (70% cocoa solids) chocolate, broken into pieces
¾ cup superfine sugar, plus extra for dusting
6 large free-range eggs, separated
1 teaspoon ground ginger

For the filling
1 cup heavy cream
1 tablespoon confectioners' sugar, sifted, plus extra for dusting

Serves 10 to 12

We all like a rolled up bit of cake but none more so than Georgie, our gorgeous recipe tester. Here she's combined soft, poached pears with a ginger spiced roulade, all held together with lightly sweetened cream. Messy and tasty (the cake, that is).

Preheat the oven to 350°F. Line a 9 x 13in jelly roll pan with parchment paper.

First poach the pears. Place the prepared pears, vanilla bean, and superfine sugar in a pan with the water. Bring to a gentle simmer and poach the pears for 15 minutes. Keep checking them—you want them to be soft but have a bit of a bite to them. When ready, drain and allow to cool.

Meanwhile make the roulade. Melt the chocolate in a microwave, or in a heatproof bowl over a pan of barely simmering water, making sure the bowl doesn't touch the water. Set aside to cool slightly.

In a large mixing bowl, whisk the sugar (reserving 1 tablespoon) with the egg yolks until pale and doubled in volume—this takes a few minutes. Stir in the melted cooled chocolate and the ground ginger.

In a separate bowl, whisk the egg whites until they form stiff peaks and add the reserved sugar. Carefully fold the egg whites into the chocolate and ginger mixture, transfer into the prepared pan, and bake for 15 minutes.

Once the roulade is cooked, remove from the oven and allow to cool in the pan. Cover with a damp kitchen towel to prevent cracking.

When you are ready to assemble, whip the cream until soft peaks form, then fold through the confectioners' sugar.

Dust a sheet of parchment paper with superfine sugar, turn the roulade onto it, and peel off the parchment paper (if you can enlist help with this, it's much easier with two). Spoon the cream over the top and scatter the pears evenly. Using the sheet of parchment paper to help you, roll up the roulade beginning from one short end. Transfer to a serving plate and serve, dusted with confectioners' sugar.

PRUE LEITH'S ULTIMATE CHOCOLATE ROULADE

Serves 8

¼ cup plus 2 tablespoons water
4½oz dark (70% cocoa solids) chocolate, broken into pieces
3½oz dark (85% cocoa solids) chocolate, broken into pieces
I teaspoon strong instant coffee
5 extra-large free-range eggs, separated
¾ cup superfine sugar
⅔ cup heavy cream
Confectioners' sugar, for dusting

"Here's one of my retro recipes from the Eighties, which is now fashionable again. It's flourless and rich and it makes a great dessert."

Preheat the oven to 400°F and line a 16 x 12in baking sheet with a piece of parchment paper (don't worry if the paper overlaps the sides a bit).

Place the water, chocolate, and instant coffee in a saucepan and melt over low heat. Set aside to cool slightly.

Beat the egg yolks with all but 1 tablespoon of the sugar until light and fluffy, then slowly fold in the melted chocolate.

In a clean bowl, whisk the egg whites until they form soft peaks. Whisk in the reserved tablespoon of sugar. Using a large metal spoon, thoroughly stir a small amount of the whites into the chocolate mixture to loosen it. Gently fold in the rest of the whites and spread the mixture evenly on the lined baking sheet. Bake for 15 minutes until the top is well risen and just set.

Slide the cake on its parchment paper onto a wire rack. To prevent it from cracking, cover immediately with a damp kitchen towel and leave to cool.

Place a piece of parchment paper on a work surface and cover it with a fine layer of confectioners' sugar. Quickly turn the cake on to the paper then peel away the top layer. Trim the edges.

Whip the cream and spread it evenly over the cake. Roll up the cake, jelly roll style, using the parchment paper to help you.

Place the roulade on to a serving dish and just before serving, sift a little confectioners' sugar over the top.

OLIVE OIL CHOCOLATE CAKE

4½oz dark (70% cocoa
  solids) chocolate,
  broken into pieces
½ cup olive oil
4 extra-large free-range eggs,
  separated
¼ cup sugar

Serves 4

This simple yet interesting chocolate cake comes from the Spanish chef José Pizarro, who loves to use good-quality Spanish olive oil in his cooking. Serve with fresh fruit and vanilla ice cream for an easy and delicious dessert.

Preheat the oven to 350°F. Oil the base and sides of an 11in springform pan and line the bottom with parchment paper.

Melt the chocolate and olive oil in a heatproof bowl over a pan of barely simmering water, making sure the bowl doesn't touch the water, then set aside to cool.

Meanwhile, whisk the egg yolks and the sugar until the mixture is light, fluffy, and pale in color. Stir in the cooled chocolate.

Using an electric hand-held beater, whip the egg whites until firm peaks form. Gently fold into the chocolate mixture.

Pour the mixture into the prepared pan and bake in the preheated oven for 15 minutes.

Remove and allow to cool before demolding. The cake will deflate as it cools because it contains no flour.

Serve with ice cream and fresh fruit.

CASSATA

Serves 8

7oz dark (70% cocoa
   solids) chocolate
1lb 2oz ricotta
⅓ cup confectioners' sugar
4 tablespoons Grand
   Marnier
3½oz mixed candied
   peel, finely diced
8 squares trifle sponge cake
   (one pack)
3 tablespoons espresso
5 tablespoons unsalted butter

This Sicilian dessert is, I suppose, a sort of cross between a cheesecake and a trifle, but made in a pudding basin. Start making it either the night before you want to serve it or in the morning for an evening snack with hot coffee or tea.

Coarsely grate 2oz of the chocolate and break the remainder into pieces.

Blend together the ricotta, confectioners' sugar, and half the Grand Marnier, then fold the peel and grated chocolate into the mixture.

Cut the cake squares in half to make two thinner squares and sprinkle the remaining Grand Marnier over the cut sides.

Line a quart pudding basin with foil, allowing enough overlap to fold over and cover the surface when filled. Use enough of the cut cake squares, Grand Marnier-side inward, to line the base and sides. Fill with the ricotta mixture and then lay the rest of the sponge cake on top, cut side down. Fold the overlapping foil over the top to cover and refrigerate for a few hours to set.

You will need to ice the cake at least an hour before serving to allow it to set.

Place the remaining chocolate with the espresso in a heatproof bowl over a pan of barely simmering water, making sure the bowl doesn't touch the water and allow to melt, stirring occasionally. Cut the butter into small pieces, then blend it into the melted chocolate one piece at a time. If the mixture splits (it will look lumpy with an oil slick on the top) you can re-emulsify it in a blender or by using a stick blender until it comes together. A tablespoon or two of water may be needed to help the emulsification.

Unwrap the dessert, invert it onto a dish, remove the foil, and pour the icing over the top, using an offset spatula to smooth the sides.

Return to the fridge for at least an hour before serving.

JANE'S CHRISTMAS PUDDING

Makes about four 1-quart pudding basins, but just split into whatever bowl size you like and adjust the steaming time.

2¼lb dried fruit (use more currants than others to make dark but you can make up the total as you wish) in roughly the following quantities:
10½oz currants
7oz raisins
7oz golden raisins
3½oz prunes, pitted and chopped
3½oz candied cherries
3½oz blueberries
Enough rum (about 1 cup) to soak all the fruit overnight
14oz dark (70% cocoa solids) chocolate
½ cup ground almonds
8oz shredded suet
2¼ cups dark brown sugar

1¾ cups all-purpose flour
1 teaspoon mixed spice
1 teaspoon baking powder
½ teaspoon cinnamon
½ teaspoon nutmeg
3½ cups fresh white breadcrumbs
Pinch of salt
Juice and zest of 1 orange
5 extra-large free-range eggs, beaten
4 tablespoons dark molasses
4 tablespoons corn syrup
1 cup Guinness
1⅓ cups grated carrot
2 apples, peeled, cored, and coarsely chopped
Butter, to grease the basins

Jane Ford, a good friend, continues the tradition of Stir Up Sunday every November with her daughters, Alice and Emily. They stir up what I consider to be the best Christmas puddings I've ever tasted. Jane, for the first time, wrote down her recipe for this book (it's an amalgamation of a few, she says), to which I added some melted chocolate and some more breadcrumbs to soak it up a bit. The result is something not overtly chocolatey, but a Christmas dessert with an extra dimension and richness. An alternative, rather than an improvement, to the original.

On making the puds Jane says, "I make this in bulk because it really is no more hassle to make in quantity. The only time-consuming part is the steaming. I do this over a few days while leaving the desserts in the fridge to mature. In fact, I actually make double the quantity given in the recipe here. I also cook it in various bowl sizes to meet all requirements!"

Soak all the dried fruit in the rum overnight.

Melt the chocolate in a microwave or heatproof bowl over a pan of barely simmering water, making sure the bowl doesn't touch the water. Leave to cool.

Grease your bowls and, unless you have a double boiler, prepare your biggest lidded pans for the steaming. They should sit on a trivet or on an upturned saucer; you need to keep the boiling water at a level of about 2in up the side of the bowls.

In a huge bowl (to avoid the risk of losing a bunch on the kitchen floor), add all the ingredients, stirring thoroughly to ensure everything is combined with no patches of dry ingredients.

Share the mixture between the greased pudding bowls but do not fill them right to the top—allow a little room for the desserts to rise.

Cut a circular piece of parchment paper the circumference of the bowl and put on top of the mixture. Cut a far bigger piece of foil to cover the bowl and create a pleat in the top to allow the steam to circulate. Place the foil over the top and push down around the outside of the bowl. Tie string around the rim to hold the foil in place. If you make a little string handle across the top, it makes the task of lifting the basin in and out of the boiling water easier.

Steam large bowls over boiling water for 4 to 6 hours—you really cannot oversteam at this point; the longer you steam the richer they get, but do ensure you top off the water level from time to time. Smaller bowls may only need 2 to 3 hours.

Lift out the bowls from the pan and allow to cool. Once cooled, you can remove the foil and parchment paper and clean off the bowls which will be quite greasy after steaming. Replace with a fresh piece of parchment paper and tie new foil over the top. Keep in the fridge or a cool place until needed—once cooked, the desserts last for months. When you are ready to eat your Christmas pudding, steam again for 1 to 2 hours.

You have to do the lighting thing... light with brandy for the traditional presentation and ooh and aah moment.

Serve with your preferred sauce, brandy butter, cream—too personal to make a call on this!

BÛCHE DE NOËL

Serves 6 to 8

For the cake
½ cup cocoa
Pinch of sea salt
3 extra-large free-range eggs
⅓ cup light muscovado
  sugar
Confectioners' sugar, for
  dusting
Butter, for greasing

For the filling
3½oz dark (70% cocoa solids)
  chocolate, broken
  into pieces
13oz unsweetened
  chestnut purée
¼ cup light muscovado
  sugar
1½ teaspoons vanilla
  extract
½ cup plus 2 tablespoons
  heavy whipping cream

A bûche de Noël is the traditional dessert the French serve at Christmas and, like so much of their pâtisserie, it has potential for other celebratory occasions throughout the year. Annie Bell gave us her recipe for this very chocolatey, very festive yule log.

To make the cake, preheat the oven to 400°F. Butter a 10 x 13in jelly roll pan, line it with parchment paper, and butter the paper as well.

Sift the cocoa into a bowl and add the salt. Place the eggs and muscovado sugar in a bowl and whisk for 8 to 10 minutes, using an electric beater, until the mixture is pale and mousse-like. Lightly fold in the cocoa in two rounds. Pour the mixture into the prepared pan and smooth it using an offset spatula. Give the pan a couple of sharp taps on the work surface to eliminate any large air bubbles and bake the cake for 8 to 10 minutes, until set and springy to the touch.

Lay out a clean kitchen towel and sift over a fine layer of confectioners' sugar. Turn the cake on to it and carefully roll it up with the towel, leaving the paper in place, starting at the short end so you end up with a short, fat roll. Leave to cool for 40 to 60 minutes.

To make the filling, gently melt the chocolate in a bowl set over a pan of simmering water, then set it aside to cool to room temperature. Cream the chestnut purée, sugar, and vanilla in a food processor, then add the chocolate. Whip the cream until it forms soft peaks, and fold it into the chocolate chestnut mixture in two rounds.

Carefully unroll the cake and peel off the parchment paper. Spread with half the chocolate chestnut mousse, then roll the cake up again and transfer it to a long serving plate, seam downward. You could also line a small board with silver foil and decorate the edge. Smooth the rest of the filling over the top, then make lines along its length with a fork, swirling the ends to create a log effect, and making a few knots on the log too.

Chill the roulade for an hour; if keeping it for longer than this, loosely cover it with plastic wrap and bring it back up to room temperature for 30 minutes before eating.

Shortly before serving, shower the log with confectioners' sugar or edible glitter.

DESSERTS

DARK AND MILK CHOCOLATE MOUSSES

Milk chocolate

3½oz milk (34% cocoa solids) chocolate

4 extra-large free-range egg whites

⅓ cup confectioners' sugar, sifted

Half-and-half, to serve

Dark chocolate

3½oz dark (70% cocoa solids) chocolate or good-quality (72% cocoa solids) baking chocolate

1 cup heavy whipping cream

1½ tablespoons confectioners' sugar, sifted

1 tablespoon light brown sugar

1 tablespoon superfine sugar

Serves 4

Using grated chocolate in a mousse gives a refreshingly different texture and flavor release. These desserts have the added advantage of not needing any cooking and can be made with a bowl, a grater, a tablespoon, and a whisk. I am usually too lazy to whip by hand and resort to some help from electric beaters.

Milk Chocolate Mousse

This recipe gives an incredibly light texture but must be made within an hour of serving. It's best if you have the egg whites separated and the chocolate grated before the meal—then, when you want mousse, it will take only a few minutes to whip up.

Finely grate the chocolate. (Unless you want to lose the tips of your fingers, you will find that you won't be able to grate the whole bar, so just do as much as you can, which should be about 3¼oz. The melty end bits are for the chef.)

Whip the egg whites to soft peaks, then add the sugar and whisk until stiff and glossy.

Carefully fold in the chocolate and pour into individual glasses.

Serve with half-and-half.

Dark Chocolate Mousse

Whereas milk chocolate and egg whites work together best in the previous recipe, dark chocolate and cream is the better match here. This version can be made and served immediately or left in the fridge for a few hours, which allows the sugar topping to dissolve somewhat and the mousse to firm up.

Finely grate the chocolate (see note, opposite).

Whip the cream with the confectioners' sugar until light, fluffy, and voluminous.

Mix together all three sugars, breaking any lumps of brown sugar with your fingers.

Carefully fold the chocolate into the cream then pour into four glasses.

Sprinkle each with the mixture of sugar and either serve immediately or chill for a few hours until required.

MARBLED MOUSSE

Serves 6

4½oz dark (70% cocoa solids)
   chocolate, finely chopped,
   plus extra shavings
   to decorate
4½oz white chocolate,
   finely chopped
4 extra-large free-range eggs,
   separated
⅓ cup superfine sugar
1⅓ cups heavy cream

You will also need six 8oz wine
   glasses

At the Green & Black's offices, we're proud to display several glass trophies from the *Good Housekeeping* Awards, as voted for by their readers. (Most recently: Favorite Organic Brand.) The *Good Housekeeping* team shared three fabulous recipes for the book, and we couldn't choose between them—so you'll also want to try the GH Chocolate and Pecan Pie, on p. 94, and the Chocolate Iced Mille Feuilles, on p. 170. (And maybe hit the gym afterward...)

Melt 3½oz of the dark chocolate in a heatproof bowl over a pan of barely simmering water, making sure the bowl doesn't touch the water. Remove from the heat and set aside to cool for 15 minutes. Meanwhile, using the same method, melt 3½oz of the white chocolate.

Place the egg yolks into one large bowl and the whites in another. Using electric beaters, whisk the yolks with the sugar for about 5 minutes until pale and mousse-like. In another bowl, using the same beaters, whip the cream until just holding its shape. Wash and dry the beaters, then whisk the egg whites until stiff but not dry.

Using a large metal spoon, fold the cream into the yolk and sugar mixture, followed by the egg whites. Spoon half the mixture into one of the now-empty bowls. Fold the cooled and melted dark chocolate and remaining chopped white chocolate into one bowl of mixture, then stir the melted and cooled white chocolate and remaining chopped dark chocolate into the other.

Spoon one mousse on top of the other and lightly fold the two together to achieve a marbled effect. Divide the mixture among six glasses. Cover and chill for 4 hours or overnight.

Top with chocolate shavings before serving.

5-MINUTE CHOCOLATE POT

7oz dark (70% cocoa solids) chocolate, chopped
⅓ cup boiling water
1 teaspoon vanilla extract
½ cup heavy whipping cream

Serves 6

Sylvain Jamois has picked up many recipes as his time as a chef, and insists this is the easiest, quickest, most impressive chocolate pot he's found. He does suggest, however, that you make it before your guests arrive so they don't feel cheated that you spent so little time and effort on their dessert.

Melt the chocolate in a microwave or heatproof bowl over a pan of barely simmering water, making sure the bowl doesn't touch the water. Take off the heat.

Add the hot water (you can use the water from the bain-marie) to the chocolate and vanilla extract. The water must be added slowly and gradually to keep the chocolate from splitting.

Add the heavy whipping cream—the texture should be like that of crème anglaise. Pour straight into espresso cups and leave to set in a cool part of the kitchen for at least 45 minutes before serving.

Tips
~ Why not vary the chocolate flavor by using one bar of dark (70% cocoa solids) and one bar of milk, espresso, or maya gold instead?
~ Assuming that you have had to buy more cream than called for, the remaining cream can be whipped and added to the top of each chocolate pot.

TIRAMISU

Serves 2

I extra-large free-range
   egg yolk
I tablespoon superfine
   sugar
¼ cup mascarpone cheese
2½oz heavy whipping cream
6 ladyfingers
¼ cup espresso
I tablespoon marsala
¾oz dark (85% cocoa
   solids) chocolate, grated

It is difficult to improve on such a classic dessert (although the 85% dark shavings on top give it an extra chocolate hit) but I thought it would be nice to have a recipe that would be ideal for a romantic night in, so this one makes just two portions. You can obviously scale up for larger numbers.

Mix the egg yolk and sugar together with a whisk until light and fluffy, then gently fold through the mascarpone.

In a separate bowl, whip the cream until soft peaks form and fold into the mascarpone mixture.

Place a spoonful of the mixture in two wine glasses or trifle dishes. Dip the ladyfingers in the espresso and arrange on top of the cream, splash the marsala over the top.

Spoon the remaining mixture over the top and finish by sprinkling with grated chocolate.

Refrigerate for 20 minutes to set before serving.

WHITE CHOCOLATE AND PASSION FRUIT DELICE

For the mousse

2 extra-large free-range
  egg yolks
¼ cup superfine sugar
¾ cup milk
7oz white chocolate
¾ cup heavy cream

For the bavarois

24 fresh passion fruit
  (you need ⅔ cup
  of juice)
2 tablespoons milk
4 sheets of gelatin,
  cut into small strips
3 extra-large free-range
  egg yolks
⅓ cup superfine sugar
½ cup heavy whipping cream

Serves 6 to 10

I love the vanilla hit of our white chocolate but, as the only cocoa element of it is cocoa butter (as in all white chocolate) it lacks the bitterness and acidity from the cocoa mass. I personally find it a bit too sweet. For this reason this recipe, from Thiery Laborde, is one of my favorites in the book as it changes my view of white chocolate. The acidity of the passion fruit cuts through the sweetness of the white chocolate brilliantly and the two layers – one a light mousse, the other a firmer bavarois – give a great combination of textures, especially with the added crunch of the passion fruit seeds.

First, make the mousse. Whisk together the yolks and sugar until light and fluffy. Heat the milk to boiling point and gradually pour onto the egg mixture, whisking constantly. Return the mixture to the saucepan and cook over low heat until it is thick enough to coat the back of a spoon. Pour this custard into a bowl, cover the surface with plastic wrap to keep a skin from forming, and set aside to cool.

Melt the chocolate in a heatproof bowl over a pan of barely simmering water, making sure the bowl doesn't touch the water, then set aside to cool. Whip the heavy cream until fairly stiff. Blend the chocolate into the cooled custard, then carefully fold in the whipped cream. Pour into a mold or individual serving dishes and leave to set in the fridge for about 1 hour.

Next make the bavarois. Reserving 3 to 4 passion fruits, halve the rest. Scrape the pulp into a fine sieve placed over a bowl or measuring cup. Separate the juice and seeds by stirring with a wooden spoon. You will need to collect ⅔ cup of juice for the next stage.

Put the milk and gelatin in a small saucepan and leave so that the gelatin soaks and softens in the cold milk: do not heat yet. Whisk together the yolks and sugar until light and fluffy, then gradually add the passion fruit juice. Whip the cream until it forms soft peaks. Gently heat the milk and stir until the gelatin has completely dissolved. Pour the milk and gelatin onto the egg mixture and stir to blend, then fold in the whipped cream. When combined, pour the cold mousse on top and return to the fridge for at least 4 hours to set.

Serve topped with the fruit pulp from the reserved passion fruit.

CHOCOLATE LIQUORICE DELICE WITH COCOA CHILE WAFER

For the delice
⅓ cup free-range egg yolks
⅔ cup superfine sugar
1½ cups whole milk
1⅓ cups heavy cream
9oz dark (70% cocoa
   solids) chocolate,
   broken into pieces
2 tablespoons liquorice paste

For the cocoa chile wafer
3 tablespoons butter
1¼ tablespoons corn syrup
1 tablespoon cabernet
   sauvignon vinegar
¼ cup superfine sugar

1½ tablespoons cocoa powder
¼oz pectin
½oz dark (70% cocoa
   solids) chocolate
¼ teaspoon sea salt
¼ teaspoon sweet smoked
   paprika (optional)
¼ teaspoon red chile flakes

To serve
1¾ cups whipped cream
3 pink grapefruit,
   segmented

Serves 6

The idea for this dessert came to Anna Hansen after a visit to her lovely Aunty Kimmi in Denmark: "I already had piece of liquorice in my mouth, then greedily stuffed in a piece of chocolate! The result was a taste sensation that I've never forgotten and one that I've since based several desserts around, this being one of them. My chocolate liquorice ice cream is also a favorite! Don't be put off this dessert even if you don't like liquorice. For some reason, this combination of liquorice and chocolate has won over the most hardened liquorice critics. If you can't find liquorice paste, use 1oz finely chopped liquorice, simmered gently in ½ cup water. It will need a lot of stirring and occasional squishing against the side of the pan."

For the delice, whisk together the egg yolks and sugar. Heat the milk and cream to boiling point then slowly pour onto the egg mixture, whisking constantly. Return the mixture to the saucepan and over a medium heat, stir constantly with a wooden spoon or spatula in a figure 8 for approximately 5 minutes until thickened. Remove from the heat and add the chocolate and liquorice paste, whisking until completely melted and incorporated. Pass the custard through a fine sieve, then press a piece of parchment paper gently on to the surface to prevent a skin from forming and leave to cool. Once cool, put the custard in the fridge for at least 2 hours, but preferably overnight.

To make the wafer, preheat the oven to 350°F. Melt the butter, corn syrup, and vinegar in a small saucepan. Add the sugar, cocoa, and pectin and bring to a boil. Continue to boil for 2 minutes, stirring occasionally. Remove from the heat and whisk in the remaining ingredients. Using an offset spatula, spread the mixture as thinly as possible on a baking sheet lined with silicone paper. The mixture will look gloopy but don't worry; it will spread as it bakes. Bake for 9 minutes, then remove from the oven and sprinkle a little more salt on top. Cool, then gently break the wafer into large chunks. It can be stored layered with parchment paper in an airtight container until needed. If the wafer mix is not crispy when cool, return the sheet to the oven for an additional few minutes.

Place a spoonful of the chocolate liquorice delice on to each serving plate. Lay a shard of wafer on top and then a spoonful of whipped cream. Scatter the grapefruit segments around the delice and serve immediately.

CHOCOLATE, CRANBERRY, AND PISTACHIO LAYERED POT

7oz cranberries
⅓ cup superfine sugar
1 tablespoon water
3oz dark (70% cocoa
  solids) chocolate
½ cup heavy whipping cream
1¼ tablespoons confectioners'
  sugar
⅓ cup shelled pistachios
2oz Graham crackers
3 tablespoons unsalted butter,
  melted

Serves 6

This is a good one to make with any (homemade) cranberry sauce left over from a Christmas turkey dinner. However, it is not difficult to stew a few cranberries any time of year, and they are easy to find frozen. This should definitely be served in individual glasses to show off the different colored layers.

Stew the cranberries with the sugar and water until soft but not collapsed. Set aside to cool.

Coarsely grate or finely chop the chocolate.

Whip the cream with the confectioners' sugar until light, fluffy, and voluminous.

Process the pistachios in a food processor until they resemble fine breadcrumbs. Add the Graham crackers and continue to process until they are the same.

Mix the melted butter into the nut mixture.

To assemble, put about 1½ tablespoons of the nut mixture into each glass, followed by a single layer of cranberries, then about 1½ tablespoons of the whipped cream, and finally a good layer of the grated chocolate so that the cream is well covered.

Chill for at least an hour before serving.

CHOCOLATE AND COCONUT RICE PUDDING

Serves 2 to 4

½ cup short grain or arborio rice
1 (14oz) can coconut milk
2 tablespoons fresh grated coconut
⅓ to ⅔ cup milk (as needed)
2oz milk chocolate (or dark 70% cocoa solids chocolate if you prefer), broken into pieces
2 tablespoons sugar (optional)

The very first recipe leaflet for Green & Black's featured Linda McCartney's brownie recipe. Craig had helped American-born Linda convert her family's recipe, which originally used unsweetened chocolate, so that it worked beautifully with G & B's, which she could find in Europe. The family still follows that brownie recipe today—and Linda's (grown-up) children, who Craig and Jo happen to know, still use Green & Black's when they're whipping up any chocolate goodies. Photographer and mother of three sons, Mary McCartney, is as savvy a cook as Linda was—and came up with this yummy dessert especially for this book.

In a medium pan, mix together the rice and coconut milk and slowly heat up so that the mixture gently simmers. Then add the coconut, stirring often. Add milk a little at a time if you feel the mixture is getting too thick.

Once the rice is nearly cooked through—approximately 15 minutes—add in the broken-up milk chocolate pieces. Stir well until the chocolate has melted in. Taste, and if you'd like it a little sweeter, add one or two tablespoons of sugar and stir well. Serve hot.

Tip
~ If you're feeling decadent, melt a little extra chocolate and swirl it through before serving.

WHITE CHOCOLATE AND CARDAMOM RICE PUDDING WITH MARMALADE AND COINTREAU SAUCE

Serves 4

½ cup short grain rice
⅓ cup golden baker's sugar
1⅓ cups 1% milk
½ cup half-and-half
3 whole cardamom pods,
  seeds removed and ground
  to a powder
3½oz white chocolate, grated

For the sauce
⅓ cup marmalade
⅓ cup Cointreau

Charles Worthington is an award-winning hairdresser, a world-class host—at his homes in the South of France, London, and Kent—and a great fan of Green & Black's, going back to the very early days when Jo Fairley (wearing her other "hat" as a Beauty Editor), introduced him to the chocolate. This is one of Charles's favorite chocolate indulgences.

Place the rice and sugar into a medium saucepan, then pour in the milk and half-and-half. Add the cardamom powder.

Bring to a boil, then lower the heat and simmer for 15 to 20 minutes, until the rice is swollen and tender. Add a little hot water if it's looking a little dry.

Remove from the heat and stir in the grated white chocolate. Cover the pan and set aside.

To make the sauce, combine the marmalade with the Cointreau and heat gently in a pan.

Divide the rice pudding between four bowls and drizzle with the sauce.

Serve decorated with a few shavings of white chocolate, if desired.

SPICED CHOCOLATE CREAM

Serves 6

1 cup heavy cream, plus
  a little extra as necessary
½ small fresh red chile,
  seeded
1 cinnamon stick
2 star anise
4 cloves
7oz dark (70% cocoa
  solids) chocolate, broken
  into pieces
Nutmeg
Shortbread cookies, for
  dipping

Mark Sargeant, a great chef who's worked with the likes of Gordon Ramsay, has given us this traditional but elegant dessert. His chocolate cream is essentially a ganache made with extra cream to make it softer and more spoonable. Infusing the spices in the hot cream is the best way to extract the flavor without them becoming overpowering.

Put the cream, chile, cinnamon stick, star anise, and cloves in a heavy-bottomed saucepan and slowly bring to a boil. Remove from the heat and leave to infuse for 20 minutes.

Strain the cream through a strainer into a measuring cup. Discard the spices and top off the hot cream to 1 cup with a little extra cream if you find the level has gone down slightly. Return to the pan, bring back to a boil, and add the chocolate, stirring off the heat until it is a velvety smooth texture.

Divide the mixture between six cups or glasses and grate a little nutmeg over the top. Serve warm or at room temperature with shortbread cookies to dip in.

CHOCOLATE CHERRY TRIFLE

Serves 6

For the custard

4 extra-large free-range egg yolks
¼ cup superfine sugar
2 tablespoons all-purpose flour
1 cup plus 2 tablespoons whole milk
3oz dark (70% cocoa solids) chocolate, chopped finely

For the topping

½ cup slivered almonds
1½ tablespoons confectioners' sugar
1 teaspoon rum

1oz dark (70% cocoa solids) chocolate

For the base

8 pieces trifle sponge cake
3½oz cherry jelly
4 tablespoons rum, preferably golden
14oz pitted cherries (use frozen out of season)

1⅓ cups heavy whipping cream
¼ cup confectioners' sugar
1 teaspoon vanilla extract

I chose cherries as the fruit element of this trifle as they go so well with chocolate and I've caramelised the almonds on the top to give them a better crunch. The other essential part is a good, thick chocolate custard. The assembled combination of sponge, alcohol, cherries, chocolate custard, cream, and almonds is so dirty and indulgent you should feel ashamed scoffing every mouthful.

First make the custard to give it time to cool. Whisk together the egg yolks and sugar then sift in the flour and whisk that in. Heat the milk to boiling point then pour onto the egg mixture, whisking constantly. Return the mixture to the saucepan and bring to a boil over low heat, still whisking. When it comes to a boil, continue to whisk constantly for another 5 minutes, still over the low heat. It will be thick and smooth. Remove from the heat and add the chocolate, whisking until fully melted and incorporated. Pour into a bowl, cover the surface with plastic wrap to prevent a skin from forming, and leave to cool.

Make the almond topping. Preheat the oven to 300°F and line a baking sheet with parchment paper. Mix the almonds, confectioners' sugar, and rum in a bowl then spread them out evenly on the sheet. Caramelize in a preheated oven until golden brown; this takes about 6 minutes, but you should be able to smell when they are ready. Remove and set aside to cool.

Split the sponges and sandwich each one with cherry jelly. Line a glass bowl or dish with the sponge sandwiches and drizzle the rum on top. Distribute the cherries evenly over the sponge cake.

Whip the cream with the confectioners' sugar and vanilla. Fold about a quarter into the cooled chocolate custard. Spoon the custard over the cherries and then the rest of the cream over the custard. Sprinkle the almonds and grate the chocolate over the top.

Chill until it's time for dessert!

RUM AND RAISIN CHOCOLATE DIPLOMAT

¾ cup raisins
About 1 cup dark rum
3½oz dark (70% cocoa
  solids) chocolate
1 cup heavy cream
½ cup half-and-half
1 tablespoon superfine sugar
½ cup whole milk
7oz ladyfingers
  (about two packages)
7oz Praline (see p. 140)

Serves 10

I love an old-school dessert done properly. This may look at home on a sweet trolley in a 1970s-themed restaurant, but this shouldn't keep you from making it. I've always been a fan of the rum and raisin combination and find that recipes that juxtapose different textures as well as flavors—in this case soft, liquor-soaked ladyfingers, chewy raisins, light, creamy chocolate, and crunchy, nutty, sweet praline—are well worth the effort.

The night before, soak the raisins in ⅓ cup of the rum and refrigerate overnight.

The following day, melt the chocolate in a microwave or heatproof bowl over a pan of barely simmering water, making sure the bowl doesn't touch the water. Set aside to cool.

Put the heavy cream, half-and-half, and the sugar into a large bowl and whip until the mixture is starting to stiffen but is still very light. Blend in the cooled chocolate. Set aside.

Pour the rum from the soaked raisins into a measuring cup and top off with extra rum as necessary to make ½ cup. Add the milk to the rum. Put this mixture in a small flat-bottomed dish such as a soup plate.

Dip the ladyfingers, one at a time, plain side down, into the rum mixture, making sure they soak up some of the liquid. Be careful not to make them too soggy, as they will absorb more liquid as they sit in the cake. Form a layer of soaked ladyfingers, tightly packed, in the base of a 9in springform pan. Don't be afraid to break up some fingers to fill in the odd gaps. Sprinkle half the raisins on top.

Cover this layer with half of the chocolate cream, spread over smoothly, and sprinkle some of the praline on top. Repeat the layers once more and finish with a thicker layer of praline. Refrigerate for a few hours before serving or freeze (see tip).

Tips

~ *If you don't have time to soak the raisins overnight, you can speed up the method by simmering the raisins in rum until they have absorbed enough liquid and look plump. The only down side is that you will need more rum as lots of it will evaporate in cooking.*

~ *The diplomat can be frozen. To keep it from drying out, make sure you wrap it well with plastic wrap before freezing. If frozen, allow to come to room temperature before serving.*

~ *Depending on how soft you want the overall texture to be, you may need more or less of the dipping mix. If you do need more, use 2 parts rum to 1 part heavy cream and 1 part milk.*

For the Praline (makes 1lb)

½lb almonds
1¼ cups sugar
3 tablespoons water
Few drops of lemon juice

Place the almonds on a baking sheet lined with parchment paper. Toast them in the oven at 325°F for 10 minutes; they should get a little color and look slightly oily when they come out. Make sure they are evenly spread out on the parchment paper.

Put the sugar and water and lemon juice in a heavy-bottomed saucepan and cook over medium heat. Stir continuously until the sugar has melted and in time starts to caramelize. Once the caramel has reached a deep amber color, pour it over the nuts and leave to cool down.

When the caramel has set, peel it away from the parchment paper and break it into chunks.

Tips
~ Have a pastry brush in a glass of water ready to brush away the crystals that will grow on the side of the pan. These must be brushed back as they will encourage more crystals to grow, resulting in a great big lump in the middle of the pan.
~ Stored in an airtight container, it will keep for a long time.
~ Most recipes will tell you to put the praline in a food processor, but crush it in a mortar and pestle if you can, as you will have better control of the texture and size of the pieces.

MILLE FEUILLES

Serves 4 to 6

8oz all-butter puff pastry
1 extra-large free-range egg,
 beaten
3½oz dark (70% cocoa
 solids) chocolate,
 broken into pieces
3 tablespoons hot water
1 vanilla bean, split lengthwise
⅔ cup heavy whipping cream
2 tablespoons confectioners' sugar
Hot water
Lemon juice, to taste

As I'm sure you're aware, this name refers to the thousand sheets or leaves the puff pastry creates. It is easy to buy ready-made all-butter puff pastry now, so there is no excuse not to make this. Satisfyingly messy to eat, leaving your lips and face a car crash of cream, chocolate, and flakes of pastry.

Preheat the oven to 350°F.

Roll out the pastry on a lightly floured surface into a rectangle about ⅛in thick, then cut it into three equal rectangles, trimming appropriately.

Place the pieces on a non-stick baking sheet and brush with the egg wash.

Bake for 15 to 20 minutes until well risen and golden brown. Remove from the oven and transfer to a wire rack to cool.

Melt the chocolate in a microwave or heatproof bowl over a pan of barely simmering water, making sure the bowl doesn't touch the water, then remove from the heat. Add the hot water and whisk until fully emulsified.

Scrape the vanilla seeds into the cream and whip until light and bulky.

Prepare the icing by mixing the confectioners' sugar with enough water and lemon juice to achieve an easily spreadable paste (remember that the cooked pastry is very delicate and breaks easily) with a good balance of acidity.

Take the cooled sheets of pastry and trim if necessary to make three equal rectangles. Spread the icing over one sheet.

Spread half the vanilla cream on a second sheet then drizzle on half of the chocolate sauce. With the end of a knife, gently nuzzle the chocolate into the cream. Repeat with the third pastry sheet then place on top of the second.

Finally top with the iced pastry sheet and serve.

Tip
~ This is difficult to cut so you may prefer to make individual mille feuilles by cutting the sheets into smaller rectangles after baking then proceeding as above for each.

RICK RODGERS' CHOCOLATE RICOTTA CHEESECAKE

Serves 8 to 10

For the cheesecake
2lbs whole milk ricotta cheese
9oz dark (70% cocoa solids) chocolate, chopped coarsely
2 teaspoons unflavored gelatin powder
3 tablespoons dark rum, strong brewed coffee, or water
½ cup heavy cream
⅓ cup superfine sugar
1 teaspoon vanilla extract

For the crust
¾ cup crushed graham cracker crumbs
3 tablespoons unsalted butter, melted, plus more for the pan
2 tablespoons light brown sugar
Good-quality cocoa powder, sifted, for dusting

Here is a decadent dessert that does not require the cook to turn on the oven. This makes it perfect for entertaining during hot weather, but actually, it works well at any time of the year, served with seasonal fruits such as orange or tangerine segments in the winter, or strawberries and raspberries in the summer. The flavor can be varied by substituting your favorite liqueur for the rum—try orange liqueur or kirsch.

Line a wire sieve with rinsed and wrung cheesecloth, and place the sieve over a bowl. Put the ricotta in the sieve and place three or four saucers to fit inside of the sieve on top. Let the ricotta drain for 30 minutes to remove the excess whey. Discard the drained whey in the bowl.

For the crust, brush the inside of an 8-inch springform pan with melted butter. Mix the graham cracker crumbs, 3 tablespoons melted butter, and the brown sugar together in a medium bowl. Press firmly and evenly into the pan; refrigerate while making the filling.

For the filling, melt the chocolate in a heatproof bowl over a saucepan of hot, not simmering, water, making sure the bowl doesn't touch the water. Remove the bowl from the saucepan and let cool until tepid, stirring often.

Sprinkle the gelatin over the rum/coffee/water in a ramekin or small bowl. Place the bowl over a saucepan of simmering water and stir the gelatin mixture until the gelatin dissolves, at least 2 minutes. Remove from the water and cool until tepid.

Whip the cream, superfine sugar, and vanilla in a chilled bowl with an electric mixer on high speed just until soft peaks form; set aside.

Transfer the ricotta and sugar to a food processor fitted with a metal blade. With the machine running, gradually add the chocolate, and then the gelatin. Stop the machine and pour the whipped cream mixture over the chocolate mixture. Pulse the mixture a few times, stopping to scrape down the sides of the bowl, and process until combined. Pour into the springform pan and smooth the top. Cover with plastic wrap and refrigerate until chilled and set, at least 2 hours or overnight.

To unmold the cheesecake, remove the sides of the pan. Decorate with a dusting of cocoa powder and dark chocolate shavings or curls.

To serve, use a sharp, thin knife dipped into hot water, and slice. Serve chilled.

Tip
~ To make chocolate curls, melt about 3oz dark (70% cocoa solids) chocolate in a heatproof bowl over a saucepan of simmering water, making sure the bowl doesn't touch the water. Pour the chocolate onto a flat, shiny surface that you can put in the fridge (you could use the base of a plate) and even out a ¼ inch layer of chocolate. Place the chocolate in the fridge to set for about 45 minutes (you want it hard, but not rock hard). Using a cheese slice, press down and pull the blade across the chocolate towards you. This should result in beautiful chocolate curls! (If the chocolate is too hard and brittle to make the curls, leave it at room temperature for a couple of minutes before you start.) Keep the curls in the fridge until you need them.

STRAWBERRY AND WHITE CHOCOLATE CHEESECAKE

6oz shortbread cookies
3 tablespoons unsalted butter,
    softened
9oz white chocolate
1¼ cups full-fat or
    light cream cheese
7oz fromage frais
    or crème fraîche
1⅓ cups strawberries,
    coarsely chopped

Serves 6

White chocolate and strawberries are a classic summer combination. This is a favorite of the Green & Black's team as it was supplied by Hanne Kinniburgh, one of the team's mother. For an extra hit of flavor, try using lemon shortbread cookies. Using crème fraîche rather than fromage frais gives a softer set to the topping, but it tastes very good.

Put the shortbread cookies in a plastic bag, tie loosely or seal, and smash with a rolling pin until they resemble breadcrumbs.

Mix the cookie crumbs with the softened butter and press firmly onto the base of a non-stick 8in springform pan. Refrigerate until needed.

Melt the white chocolate in a heatproof bowl over a pan of barely simmering water, making sure the bowl doesn't touch the water, then set aside to cool.

Beat together the cream cheese and fromage frais until smooth and thick. Add the strawberries to the cheese mixture with the cooled melted chocolate and mix.

Spoon the cheesecake topping onto the cookie base. Level the top and chill for 4 to 6 hours or overnight before serving.

CHOCTASTIC CHEESECAKE

Serves 12

For the base
10oz chocolate
   Graham crackers
7 tablespoons unsalted
   butter, melted

For the topping
1 cup full-fat cream
   cheese
1 large free-range egg plus
   1 large free-range egg yolk
2 drops vanilla extract
⅓ cup heavy cream
⅓ cup granulated sugar
2 tablespoons self-rising flour
2½ tablespoons good-quality
   cocoa powder
3½oz dark (70% cocoa
   solids) chocolate

To decorate
2oz dark (70% cocoa
   solids) chocolate
   (keep as a block)
1 tablespoon cocoa powder

This indulgent cheesecake recipe was given to us by The English Cheesecake Company, so we knew it was going to be a winner.

First prepare the base. Reduce the chocolate Graham crackers to crumbs in a blender or place in a strong plastic bag, loosely tie, and crush with a rolling pin. Mix the crumbs with the melted butter to form a soft consistency. Press into the bottom of a greased 8in cake pan; use the back of a spoon to help make it firm and even. Place the pan in the fridge while you make the topping.

Preheat the oven to 250°F. Put the cream cheese and eggs in a blender and mix until smooth. Add the vanilla and cream and blend until smooth. Sift together the sugar, flour, and cocoa powder and add slowly to the cream mix. Break the chocolate into pieces and scatter over the top of the biscuit base. Pour the chocolate cheesecake mix over the chocolate pieces and bake for 1 hour. Allow to cool completely in the pan.

Meanwhile, prepare the chocolate shavings. Use the whole blade of a sharp knife to scrape shavings from the surface of the chocolate bar. Distribute over the cake and, just before serving, dust with a little cocoa powder.

CHOCOLATE PANNA COTTA WITH VANILLA POACHED PEARS

For the panna cotta
1⅔ cups whole milk
¼ cup golden baker's sugar
1 teaspoon agar-agar powder (or 1 tablespoon agar-agar flakes)
1 teaspoon vanilla extract (to taste)
5½oz dark (85% cocoa solids) chocolate, broken into pieces

For the pears
2 cups water
¼ cup golden baker's sugar
1 vanilla bean, split and seeds scraped
2 ripe but firm pears

Cream, to serve (optional)

Serves 4

Naomi Knill, writer of the food blog *The Ginger Gourmand*, loves panna cotta, but often can't eat it because it is normally made with gelatin and not suitable for vegetarians (and non-meat eaters like herself). So she created this recipe using agar-agar—a vegetarian-friendly setting agent. The vanilla and pears complement the rich chocolate in the panna cotta, making it a stunning dessert that is quick and easy to prepare.

Place the milk and sugar in a saucepan and bring slowly to a boil over a low heat, stirring often to ensure the milk doesn't burn. Reduce the heat to a simmer and add the agar-agar. Whisk continuously for 3 to 4 minutes to ensure that the agar-agar dissolves (see the package instructions). Remove the pan from the heat and add the vanilla extract and dark chocolate and whisk again until the chocolate is melted and the mixture combined.

Strain the chocolate mixture through a fine sieve and pour into four individual ramekins. Cover with plastic wrap and leave to cool. Once cool, transfer to the fridge until set for at least 4 hours or overnight.

To make the poached pears, add the water, sugar, split vanilla bean and seeds to a pan, bring to a boil, and simmer gently for 5 minutes. Meanwhile, peel and halve the pears and then remove the core from each half. Place the pear halves into the poaching liqueur and simmer gently for 5 to 10 minutes until the pears are cooked but not too soft. Remove the pears from the pan with a slotted spoon and set aside to cool. (You can prepare the poached pears in advance with the panna cotta and then store in the fridge in a sealed container for 24 hours.)

To demold the panna cottas, dip each ramekin in a little boiling water for a few seconds. Place a plate over the top of the ramekin and then holding both ramekin and plate firmly, quickly invert them to release the panna cotta onto the plate. Slice the pear halves and place one on each plate with the panna cottas.

Serve the panna cottas and pears just as they are or with a little thick cream.

Tip
~ *This dessert can be made in advance and so is perfect for stress-free entertaining!*

GREEN & BLACK'S ULTIMATE CHOCOLATE FONDUE

Serves 12

A chocolate fondue has two essential parts: a thick, hot, chocolate-based sauce, and a range of complementary foods to dip into said sauce, also known as the dippables.

The Sauce

The first part to get right is the sauce. Cookbooks and the internet are littered with recipes for chocolate fondues and they seem to use a relatively large number of different ingredients other than chocolate such as sugar, corn syrup, cocoa powder, butter, cream, and evaporated milk.

In the name of research, I tried all these ingredients to see if I could understand why they were used. I made up a basic sugar syrup with sugar and water, a more complex one with water, sugar, corn syrup, and cocoa powder and added cream, butter, and evaporated milk. I had our six chocolate bars to experiment with: Dark 70%, Milk, Maya Gold, Almond, Ginger, and Mint.

In each case I found that the basic sugar syrup made everything too sweet and the one with cocoa gave a uniformity to all the chocolates, therefore losing their individual characteristics. The last main method of making a chocolate sauce uses cream and butter or evaporated milk which diluted the chocolate intensity. Why would I want to use ingredients to change the balance of sweetness and chocolate and cocoa intensity when my predecessor and I had already spent time getting the balance of these correct in the chocolate bars?

So, apart from the Dark 70%, which needs some cream to temper the natural acidity of the high level of cocoa mass, the others all just need a little water. This may sound a bit odd but I assure you it works.

Recipes

Each recipe is for a 3½oz bar of chocolate which will serve 2 to 3 people. Multiply the recipe accordingly for more people. The basic method is the same for all of them and can be heated up conventionally on the stove or in a microwave. The catch is not to overheat because chocolate can easily burn. When serving, a fondue set is ideal, but if you don't have one, then the sauce will stay pretty warm in a preheated bowl and can be zapped in a microwave for 10 seconds every now and then if needed or kept warm above a bowl of hot water. Remember, a fondue should be warm to hot, not scorching. Overheating the sauce will not only ruin the chocolate but could burn your mouth.

3½oz bar Green & Black's
  Dark 70% chocolate,
  broken into pieces
½ cup heavy cream
2 tablespoons water

Dark 70%

Conventional method

Place the chocolate pieces in a saucepan with the cream and water. Heat very gently, stirring with a small wire whisk to emulsify. If the resulting sauce is too thick, add a little water and whisk in to emulsify.

Microwave

Place the chocolate pieces in a plastic bowl with the cream and water. Give the ingredients 10-20 second bursts in the microwave, whisking in between. Do this until emulsified and warm.

3½oz bar Green & Black's
  Milk, Maya Gold, Mint,
  Ginger, or Almond
  chocolate, broken
  into pieces
3 tablespoons water

Milk, Maya Gold, or Mint

Proceed as above, but only using water to let down the chocolate.

Ginger or Almond

Drop the chocolate pieces into a food processor. Blend until the chocolate resembles fine breadcrumbs. (The reason for this is to break up the almonds or the ginger into very small pieces so they will be suspended through the sauce and not sink to the bottom. It also distributes the flavor of these pieces homogenously.) Proceed as above.

Tips for extra flavor

~ *Once you've mastered the basics, you can adapt your fondue to your taste. Below are a few suggestions for each of the Green & Black's chocolate bars:*

Ginger

Try adding freshly grated ginger, ground ginger, lemon zest, or a spoonful of honey to the fondue for extra heat, zest, or sweetness.

Maya Gold

A squeeze of orange juice, a grating of orange zest, a splash of Grand Marnier, triple sec, or Cointreau, or a spoonful of orange marmalade will all give this fondue an extra orange hit.

Almond

Adding Amaretto, an almond-flavored liqueur, will give this fondue an extra punch.

Mint

Fresh mint leaves are the best way to give this fondue an authentic, fresh flavor. Tear off a handful, throw into the fondue, and allow to infuse before serving.

Milk and Dark 70%

The simplest way to intensify the flavor of these fondues (or, in fact, any of the fondues for that matter) is to add a pinch of sea salt. A pinch of ground spice or the whole version, bruised and infused—cinnamon sticks, cardamom pods, allspice berries, a couple of dried red chiles, or a scraped vanilla bean—will give a definite twist. Try replacing the water with a shot of espresso for a mocha fondue. A spoonful of peanut butter will give a familiar, addictive taste that all ages will appreciate.

Dippables

Importantly, everyone likes something different so be sure to provide a range of dippables to satisfy all your guests. For things that can be cut up—fruit, cake, bread, etc—it's best to prepare 1in cubes or slices. These can then be dipped in using fondue forks, wooden skewers, or plain old forks. Morsels that can't be cut, such as pretzels and nuts, will have to be hand dipped and taste all the better for it. I reckon there are three main classes of things one can dip into a chocolate fondue: fruit, sweet, and savory:

Fruit

The list is almost endless, but the following are usually popular: strawberries, banana (try grilling and caramelizing slices for an extra treat), dried apricots, apple, grapes, pears, peaches, pineapples, cherries, raspberries, blackberries, and candied fruit: orange peel, lemon peel, grapefruit peel, and ginger (obviously not a fruit but candied and therefore included in this section).

Sweet

These can be homemade or store-bought. A combination of pride, time, and honesty will dictate this. Again the list is almost endless... biscotti, cookies, muffins, brownies, pastry squares (buy a pack of all-butter puff pastry, roll out, cut into 1in squares, and bake), almond macaroons, amaretti cookies, shortbread, marshmallows, and cake: ginger, chocolate, vanilla sponge, and angel food cake.

Savory

Probably my favorite: pretzels, chips, sourdough bread, salted pastry squares, salted popcorn, gorgonzola dolce (yes, a blue cheese—try it before you dismiss it), and nuts: almonds, hazelnuts, brazils, walnuts, pecans, macadamias, and peanuts (not strictly a nut—it's a legume—but best to conform to popular vernacular in these instances).

ULTIMATE CHOCOLATE SOUFFLÉ

Serves 6

For the ramekins
2 tablespoons unsalted butter
1 tablespoon good-quality cocoa powder

For the pastry cream
⅔ cup whole milk
1 whole extra-large free-range egg and 1 extra-large egg yolk
2½ teaspoons superfine sugar
1 tablespoon strong bread flour
1 teaspoon cornstarch

For the soufflé
9oz dark (70% cocoa solids) chocolate, broken into pieces
4 extra-large egg yolks
5½oz pastry cream
8 extra-large egg whites
⅓ cup superfine sugar
Pinch of cream of tartar

The G&B's team visited Adam Byatt's restaurant long before the idea for the cookbook had been conceived. One of the team had sneakily called ahead to ask if Adam would cook a special Green & Black's recipe for dessert and this was the recipe that delighted us all—not least because they all had a confectioners' sugar G&B's logo on them. When the cookbook was confirmed, we were immediately on the phone and thankfully he agreed to let us have his recipe. We like to think it was created just for us, but it was so good we think he may have done it once or twice before!

First prepare 6 x 4½oz ramekins. Melt the butter in a small saucepan and, using a pastry brush, coat the sides of the ramekins.

Add all of the cocoa powder to one ramekin, gently tip it on its side, and roll it around to evenly coat the inside with the powder. Do this over another ramekin to catch any falling cocoa powder. Once it is fully coated, empty the ramekin into the next one and, holding it upside down, gently tap it to remove any excess cocoa. Repeat the process until all the ramekins are coated, and then put them in the fridge to chill.

Next make the pastry cream. Add the milk to a heavy-bottomed saucepan and bring slowly to a boil. Whisk together the whole egg, yolk, sugar, flour, and cornstarch. Gradually pour the scalding milk over the egg mixture and whisk until smooth. Return the mixture to the saucepan and bring to a boil over low heat, whisking continuously. Continue to whisk for another 5 to 8 minutes until the mixture is thick and smooth. Remove from the heat, pass through a fine sieve into a bowl, cover the surface with plastic wrap to prevent a skin from forming, and leave to cool.

Preheat the oven to 400°F.

To make the soufflé, melt the chocolate in a heatproof bowl over a pan of barely simmering water, making sure the bowl doesn't touch the water, then set aside to cool.

Put the egg yolks into another bowl and whisk until light and fluffy. Add the cooled pastry cream, then pour in the melted chocolate and, using a plastic spatula, incorporate everything together until smooth and glossy. Set aside at room temperature.

Put the egg whites, a third of the sugar, and the cream of tartar into a clean bowl. Whisk for 5 minutes using an electric whisk. Add the remaining sugar and continue to whisk until the egg whites stand in firm peaks.

Add just over a third of the whisked egg white to the chocolate mixture and whisk vigorously until well incorporated. Very gently, using a metal spoon, fold in the remaining egg white until the mixture is glossy and free of any lumps of egg white.

Gently spoon this into the lined ramekins right to the top, then run your thumb around the rim of the mold to clean off any butter or mix from the edges (this will allow the soufflés to rise evenly).

Place the ramekins in the preheated oven and cook for 16 to 18 minutes. The soufflés will rise evenly about ¾in above the edge of the ramekin. Do not open the door during this process.

Once the soufflés are cooked (they should still be soft in the center), serve immediately.

Tips
~ Using a metal spoon to fold in the egg whites prevents too much air from being knocked out as you incorporate them into the mixture.
~ Ice cream is a great accompaniment to soufflé. Freeze little scoops of ice cream onto teaspoons and, once the soufflés are cooked, remove the spoons from the freezer and dip into the ramekins. The contrast between the hot and cold is great. If you are going to try this, make sure you put the ice cream into the soufflés at the very last minute, or let your guests do it themselves.
~ Try the following flavored ice creams to complement your chocolate soufflé: maramalade, coffee, or even good old vanilla.

MINT CHOCOLATE BOMBS

Serves 6

6oz mint chocolate
3 extra-large free-range eggs
     plus 3 extra-large free-range
     egg yolks
½ cup granulated sugar
13 tablespoons butter,
     softened, plus extra for
     greasing
⅓ cup all-purpose flour
Confectioners' sugar, for
     dusting
You will also need six
     5½oz ramekins

Lulu's son Jordan and his business partner Tim created this recipe for their restaurant, Trullo, which has just opened in London. Lulu has tried it many times and absolutely loves it, and so when Jo asked her for a contribution, she thought it would be a great addition to the book.

Preheat the oven to 350°F.

Melt the chocolate in a heatproof bowl over a pan of barely simmering water, making sure the bowl doesn't touch the water. Remove from the heat and set aside to cool.

Whisk the eggs, yolks, and sugar together until pale and mousse-like. Add the softened butter and continue to beat until incorporated. Add in the cooled melted chocolate and whisk together. Fold in the flour.

Butter the base and sides of the ramekins and place a circle of parchment paper in each to prevent the mixture from sticking. Spoon equal amounts into ramekins (to about three-quarters full) and bake for 15 minutes.

Dust with confectioners' sugar and serve with crème fraîche.

ICE CREAMS
AND MORE

SALLY CLARKE'S BITTER CHOCOLATE AND BUTTERMILK ICE CREAM

3 extra-large free-range
   egg yolks
½ cup superfine sugar
⅔ cup milk
⅔ cup heavy cream
2oz dark (70% cocoa solids),
   chocolate, grated
3½oz dark (85% cocoa
   solids) chocolate,
   grated
½ cup buttermilk

Serves 4 to 5

I remember going to Sally Clarke's shop in the early 90s when I worked in Oddbins in Kensington, London. It was one of the few places you could buy really good bread back then.

Sally's recipe uses buttermilk which is actually low in fat (it was originally what was left over after churning cream into butter), but has a certain amount of acidity in the form of lactic acid. It works very well here with the dark chocolate, to give an ice cream that is for those, like me, who don't like their "sweets" too sweet.

Sally suggests serving with plain cookies such as freshly baked *langues de chat* or vanilla shortbread.

Put the egg yolks with half the sugar in a medium bowl and whisk until light, fluffy, and pale in color. Heat the milk and cream together with the remaining sugar to just under boiling point. Pour the cream mixture into the yolks and whisk until blended. Immediately return to the pan and cook over medium heat until it begins to thicken. Do not allow to boil.

Add the grated chocolates and stir until smooth. Add the buttermilk and stir until well blended.

Strain into a chilled bowl and cool. Once cool, pour into an ice-cream maker and churn following the manufacturer's instructions. Keep in the freezer until required. It is best served within 12 hours of churning, but will keep well for at least 1 week in the freezer.

WHITE CHOCOLATE AND LEMON CHEESECAKE ICE CREAM

Serves 10

6 extra-large free-range
 egg yolks
¾ cup superfine sugar
1 vanilla bean, split
 lengthwise
½ cup whole milk
½ cup heavy whipping
 cream
½ cup good-quality
 cream cheese
Finely grated zest
 of 1 large lemon
5½oz white chocolate,
 grated

To serve
White chocolate
 (in a block)
Strawberries

Another winning way to use white chocolate's richness but adding something sour and bitter, in this case lemon zest, to balance the inherent sweetness. If you like your ice cream even more lemony, try squeezing the juice of the lemon into the mix when you add the zest.

Add the egg yolks and sugar to a medium bowl and whisk until light, fluffy, and pale in color.

Scrape the seeds from the vanilla bean into a pan with the milk and cream. Heat to just under boiling point, then whisk into the egg mixture.

Return to the pan and, using a wooden spoon, stir over low heat until the mixture thickens sufficiently to coat the back of a spoon. Do not let it boil.

Remove from the heat and allow to cool, then stir in the cream cheese and lemon zest and refrigerate until cold.

Transfer to an ice-cream maker and churn following the manufacturer's instructions.

When almost fully churned, add the grated chocolate, mix together with the ice cream, then remove and store in the freezer until needed.

To serve, use the whole blade of a sharp knife to scrape shavings from the surface of the white chocolate bar. Sprinkle over the ice cream and enjoy with juicy summer strawberries.

DARK CHOCOLATE AND CARDAMOM ICE CREAM

4½oz dark (70% cocoa
  solids) chocolate
Seeds from ½ vanilla bean
2 cardamom pods
¾ cup whole milk
⅓ cup superfine sugar
¾ cup heavy cream

Serves 6-8

Any strong spices or herbs have to be used with caution and a light touch, even with an ingredient as intensely flavored as chocolate, as the aim is to achieve balance, where everything can be tasted and nothing dominates. Richard Bertinet, of the UK's Bertinet Kitchen, has managed this superbly with his chocolate and cardamom ice cream, with a dose of vanilla seeds to add depth, complexity, and richness.

Melt the chocolate in a heatproof bowl over a pan of barely simmering water, making sure the bowl doesn't touch the water.

Split the vanilla bean lengthwise and scrape out the seeds with the back of a knife. Then crush the cardamom pods with the flat of the blade of the knife.

Place the milk in a separate pan and heat to just under boiling point, then add the sugar, vanilla seeds, and cardamom pods. Stir until the sugar is dissolved.

Using a strainer to catch the crushed cardamom pods, pour the milk into the melted chocolate and stir. Add the cream, stir well, and leave to cool at room temperature.

Once cool, pour into an ice-cream maker and churn following the manufacturer's instructions. Keep in the freezer until required.

MILK CHOCOLATE, RUM, AND RAISIN SEMI-FREDDO

Serves 6 to 8

½ cup raisins

2 tablespoons light rum

8oz milk chocolate,
broken into pieces

2 extra-large free-range eggs
plus 2 extra-large free-range
egg yolks

½ cup superfine sugar

1 teaspoon vanilla extract

1 cup plus 3 tablespoons heavy
cream, semi-whipped

2½oz cooked meringue,
crushed into small pieces

I love the old-school combination of rum and raisin and so didn't hesitate to approve this chocolatey twist on rum and raisin ice cream, offered to us by Paul Gayler, the head chef at The Lanesborough hotel in London.

Place the raisins in a small bowl, add the rum, and leave to macerate overnight.

Melt the chocolate in a heatproof bowl over a pan of barely simmering water, making sure the bowl doesn't touch the water. Set aside to cool.

Put the eggs, yolks, and sugar in a medium bowl and whisk until light, fluffy, and pale in color.

Add the melted chocolate, vanilla extract, the soaked raisins, and the rum. Mix together.

Gently fold in the semi-whipped cream and the meringue pieces.

Line a 2lb loaf pan with plastic wrap, allowing a 2in overlap around the sides.

Fill with the semi-freddo mix, then tap the pan on the work surface to release the air bubbles.

Fold over the overhanging plastic wrap to cover, then place in the freezer to freeze overnight.

To serve, turn the semi-freddo onto a plate, carefully peel away the plastic wrap, and cut into thick slices.

BAKED ALASKA

Serves 6 to 8

⅔ cup slivered almonds
1¾ tablespoons confectioners' sugar
1 teaspoon rum
1 x 8in sponge cake
A good splash of PX (Pedro Ximinez) sherry
1 pint good-quality chocolate ice cream

For the meringue

1¾ cups superfine sugar
1½ tablespoons corn syrup
¼ cup plus 1 tablespoon water
6 extra-large free-range egg whites
A teaspoon of vanilla extract

I urge you to try this recipe as it is much simpler than you might expect, especially if you buy the sponge cake base (a bit of a cheat, but you are going to douse it in rich, raisiny, alcoholic Pedro Ximinez sherry) and the chocolate ice cream. The egg whites of the meringue are cooked by the hot sugar syrup so the meringue needs no further cooking, just a good blast from a blowtorch to brown it.

First make the almond topping. Preheat the oven to 350°F and line a baking sheet with parchment paper. Mix the almonds, confectioners' sugar, and rum in a bowl then spread them out evenly on the sheet. Caramelize in the oven until golden brown; this takes about 6 minutes, but you should be able to smell when they are ready. Remove and set aside to cool.

Sit the sponge cake on a large plate (cut to size if need be) and sprinkle with a few tablespoons of PX sherry until nicely covered up but in no way soaking.

Remove the ice cream from the freezer and put in the fridge to soften a little.

To make the meringue, gently heat the superfine sugar, corn syrup, and water until the sugar is dissolved. Increase the heat and, using a sugar thermometer, boil until the syrup reaches about 225°F. At this point, beat the egg whites in an electric stand mixer or with a hand-held mixer until stiff. Remove the syrup from the heat when the thermometer reads 250°F. Turn the mixer to its lowest setting and beat the whites while pouring in the syrup in a thin stream. Once all the syrup is incorporated, add the vanilla extract to the mixture and continue to beat until cold.

Now remove the ice cream from the fridge and scoop into the center of the sponge cake leaving a 1-inch border around the ice cream. Sprinkle the ice cream with the caramelized almonds then smother everything with the meringue, ensuring it entirely covers the sponge cake and all the ice cream, leaving no gaps. An offset spatula can be useful here. Fire up your blowtorch and color the meringue all over.

Serve immediately with a glass of lightly chilled PX.

ULTIMATE CHOCOLATE SAUCE

½ cup heavy cream
¼ cup whole milk
3½oz dark (70% cocoa
    solids) chocolate,
    broken into pieces

Makes just over 1 cup

The beauty of this sauce is that the balance of ingredients means that it can be used hot (freshly made), cold (direct from the fridge), or any temperature in between. If used from the fridge it just needs a good stir to get moving and make it pourable. Like all good food, it's also incredibly simple and relies on tasty, honest ingredients.

Pour the cream and milk into a small saucepan and bring to a boil.

Remove from the heat, add the chocolate, and whisk until smooth and all the chocolate is melted.

Serve hot, warm, at room temperature, or cold from the fridge.

CHOCOLATE ICED MILLE FEUILLES

7oz dark (70% cocoa solids) chocolate, broken into pieces

10½oz white chocolate, broken into pieces

1½ cups heavy cream

2 teaspoons vanilla extract

2 large free-range egg whites

¼ cup confectioners' sugar

Cocoa powder, for dusting

Serves 12

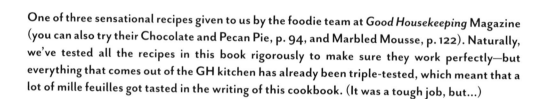

One of three sensational recipes given to us by the foodie team at *Good Housekeeping* **Magazine (you can also try their Chocolate and Pecan Pie, p. 94, and Marbled Mousse, p. 122). Naturally, we've tested all the recipes in this book rigorously to make sure they work perfectly—but everything that comes out of the GH kitchen has already been triple-tested, which meant that a lot of mille feuilles got tasted in the writing of this cookbook. (It was a tough job, but...)**

Use a little water to dampen a 2lb loaf pan, then line with a double layer of plastic wrap. Cut out two sheets of parchment paper, each 18 x 13in, and place on separate baking sheets.

Melt the dark chocolate in a heatproof bowl over a pan of barely simmering water, making sure the bowl doesn't touch the water. Spoon half the melted chocolate on to each sheet of parchment and spread it to the edges in a thin layer. Transfer the baking sheets to the fridge and chill for 30 minutes.

Put the white chocolate into a second bowl with ½ cup of the cream, then melt slowly over a pan of simmering water, as above. Set aside to cool.

In a separate bowl, whip the remaining cream with the vanilla extract until just holding its shape. Fold into the cooled melted white chocolate.

Whisk the egg whites in a spotlessly clean bowl and gradually whisk in the confectioners' sugar. Fold them into the white chocolate mixture.

Peel the dark chocolate from the parchment and break into large pieces. Put a quarter of them into a freezerproof container for decoration.

Spoon a quarter of the cream mixture into the lined pan and layer with a third of the remaining dark chocolate pieces. Repeat the layers twice more, and finish with a final layer of cream mixture.

Cover with plastic wrap and freeze, along with the reserved chocolate, overnight or for up to a month.

An hour before serving, transfer the mille feilles and reserved chocolate to the fridge. Turn on to a serving plate and carefully peel away the plastic wrap. Break the reserved chocolate into smaller jagged pieces and arrange on top. Dust with cocoa powder to serve.

CHOCOLATE PARFAIT

Serves 6 to 8

⅔ cup superfine or
   granulated sugar
½ cup water
4½oz dark (70% cocoa
   solids) chocolate,
   broken into pieces
4 extra-large free-range
   egg yolks
I tablespoon Armagnac
I tablespoon espresso
I cup heavy whipping
   cream

If you like frozen desserts, then this is the one for you. The rich ingredients are offset by the temperature at which you serve it—straight from the freezer—giving a dense, rich, but incredibly clean-tasting dessert.

Combine the sugar with the water in a pan and boil until fully dissolved, then boil for another 3 minutes.

Remove from the heat, add the chocolate, and stir until it has melted and is fully emulsified.

Whisk the egg yolks until they are pale, then slowly pour in the chocolate mixture, continuing to whisk until the mixture has cooled. You'll need electric beaters or the whisk attachment on an electric mixer for this. Add the Armagnac and espresso and whisk until fully emulsified.

Whip the cream until light and fluffy then fold into the chocolate mixture.

Pour into individual ramekins and freeze.

SWEETS AND TREATS

TEMPERING CHOCOLATE

In our first book, we gave an accurate but relatively technical method for tempering chocolate involving quite a lot of equipment and the need for accurate temperature readings. This sort of method is needed if you start with untempered chocolate but, as all chocolate available to buy is already tempered, I thought it would be good to give a much easier method when using pre-tempered chocolate.

The science bit

Cocoa butter, the fat element of cocoa, melts just below body temperature. Its function in a bar of chocolate is to coat all the particles—non-fat cocoa solids, sugar, milk sugars, and milk proteins (dependent on which type of chocolate)—and allow it to melt easily in the mouth. Cocoa butter has six different cocoa butter forms, some of which are unstable since they melt at low temperatures, and others that are stable. Tempering chocolate is essentially heating, then cooling, then heating the chocolate—all while stirring it—to set a small amount of stable cocoa butter crystals, which then spread throughout the rest of the chocolate to set it with a good snap, a shine, and to ensure it won't be sticky. The theory behind the easy tempering detailed below is that you heat the pre-tempered chocolate until it is only just melted, at which point there are still some cocoa butter crystals, which are enough of a seed to allow the chocolate to set properly when cooled.

Easy tempering

I find that this works best in a plastic container in a microwave; it is quicker and it saves both cleaning up and time. However, the same process can be done in a bowl suspended over a saucepan of hot water—just remember to take the bowl off the heat when there is a small amount of chocolate that is still unmelted, and then stir the chocolate to melt the final little pieces.

Break up the required amount of chocolate and put it in a plastic container such as a large measuring cup. Start by giving the chocolate bursts of 30 seconds, stirring between each burst. When the chocolate starts to melt, reduce the time of bursts to 20 or 10 seconds and finally 5 seconds. The time you give the chocolate depends on the amount of chocolate you are trying to temper and the strength of your microwave. The aim is to stop heating the chocolate when there is still a small amount of chocolate unmelted. The final melting can be done by stirring the chocolate. At this point, it should feel slightly cool when you test a dipped finger against your lips (your lips are very sensitive to temperature and make a great natural thermometer). If you've overheated the chocolate and the chocolate feels warm against your lips (I mean slightly overheated... If you have burnt the chocolate, then you have to throw it away, but this shouldn't happen if you pay attention), all is not lost. Add a few more pieces of tempered chocolate to the melted chocolate and stir. Keep feeling the temperature against your lips until it feels slightly cool.

To test if the chocolate is tempered before using it, I usually drizzle a little onto a marble surface. Within a couple of minutes, the chocolate should have turned slightly matte and have hardened a bit. Alternatively, you can drizzle a little onto a piece of foil or parchment paper and stick it in the fridge for a minute or so. If it doesn't set, it will still be too warm with not enough/any seed crystals, so more chocolate will need to be added and stirred into it until the temperature is brought down. If the chocolate is tempered and there are still a few lumps of chocolate in the mix, just fish them out.

The beauty of this method is that you don't need a lot of equipment or need to know the different temperatures different chocolates need to be cooled and then heated up to. It works for all colors of chocolate and for any amount of chocolate. The more often you do it the faster you become because you will understand the best times to use with your microwave and will be less likely to overheat the chocolate. I hope you enjoy experimenting with this method. It is the one I use most often in my kitchen.

CHOCOLATE BARS-
THE ONES THAT GOT AWAY

Over the last eleven years I've been lucky enough to see a large number of chocolate bars I've developed be launched (and other products including boxes of chocolate, ice cream, cookies, and Easter eggs) and be successful. I still get a big thrill when someone says how much they like a certain flavor I've worked on.

Unfortunately, not all bar flavors make it to the store shelves, and this can be for a number of reasons. All the organic ingredients we use are the highest quality we can find, but some are just too expensive to be able to put the chocolate bars out at an affordable price. Some we cannot source organically. Others do not physically work in the factory or the ingredient does not remain of a high enough quality during its shelf life (try and guess which was which).

So I thought I'd give you a few ideas of chocolate bars that never made it, but still taste great. You can make these yourself if you temper the chocolate according to the instructions on page 176, then just mix in the ingredients and pour the well-stirred mixture onto a piece of parchment paper (most of us don't have a handy chocolate mold hanging around in the kitchen). You can leave it in a large

circle or get the back of a spoon or an offset spatula and coax it into your desired shape. We cool our chocolate at around 60°F, but a cool pantry or a fridge will do the job well. Just remember not to put the chocolate near strong smelling foods—the chocolate will absorb the flavor remarkably quickly. Once the tempered chocolate has set hard, wrap it in plastic wrap and store wherever you usually keep your chocolate (ideally between 60°F and 68°F but, let's face it, where would that be in the average house?).

When I refer to milk chocolate, I would ideally use our 37% milk baking chocolate, but the 34% milk chocolate works well too (it's just a little viscous). With the dark bars, I tend to use a 60% cocoa-solids dark chocolate that we make specially for dark chocolate bars with ingredients in them (it seems to give a slightly better balance than the 70%) but, since this is not widely available, I would recommend the 70% dark chocolate. Lastly, calculate how much chocolate you need in each recipe by working back from the added ingredient and the percentage you need, e.g., if you have 3½oz of dates then you'll need 10½oz of tempered chocolate to make a sizable 14oz bar.

Milk chocolate and medjool dates
Chop the dates into approximately ½in chunks (this is sticky business). Temper the chocolate, mix in the chopped dates (about 25% dates, 75% milk chocolate), and pour onto the parchment paper.

Dark chocolate with nougat
Try and find a bar of hard Italian nougat called torrone (it often has almonds in it; you can usually purchase it in speciality stores or online). Before unwrapping it, have at it with a rolling pin or similar, smashing it up like you mean business. You are aiming for ¼in to ½in chunks. Continue as above using around 20% nougat to 80% dark chocolate.

Milk chocolate with caramelized, salted popcorn
Pop the popcorn in the usual manner, but be sure you don't eat it all first! Allow to cool. Heat 3½oz of sugar and a splash of water in a heavy-bottomed pan, allow to dissolve, then continue cooking until it reaches 245°F (you will need a candy thermometer for this). Add three or four handfuls of the popcorn (this depends on how big your pan is; you want it to be quite full but not so much that it will go everywhere when you stir it) to the sugar syrup and mix well until the sugar has crystallized and sticks to the popcorn. Pour onto a piece of parchment paper and, when cool enough to handle, separate the stuck together popcorn as well as you can. Heat the popcorn in a non-stick pan, stirring continuously. The sugar on the popcorn will begin to caramelize. Continue to cook until well caramelized all over but be careful not to burn the sugar and make it bitter (this can happen very quickly). Just before it is ready, sprinkle in some salt to taste (I tend to use quite a bit of sea salt to cut through the sweetness of the caramel). Empty the caramelized popcorn onto parchment paper and once again separate if necessary and allow to cool. Continue as above using approximately 10% popcorn to 90% milk chocolate.

Dark chocolate with pistachios
Quite simply, buy the best, greenest, most fragrant pistachios you can get your hands on and use about 25% with 75% dark chocolate. If you wish, you can use the roasted, salted kind.

SIX HOT
CHOCOLATE
RECIPES

All recipes serve one

1 tablespoon water
3 teaspoons good-quality
  drinking chocolate
  granules
¾oz dark (70% cocoa solids)
  chocolate, broken into
  small pieces
⅓ cup ruby port

Dark Chocolate Wine

This recipe is inspired by one developed in 1726 by pastry chef John Nott at Syon House in southwest London, the London home of the Duke of Northumberland.

Add the water, chocolate granules, and chocolate in a small saucepan and heat gently, stirring or whisking constantly to prevent burning and help the ingredients to emulsify. Once a smooth paste has been achieved, add the port and whisk together to blend all the ingredients. Pour into an appropriate glass, chill for 30 minutes, and serve cool.

¾ cup milk
10 fresh mint leaves,
   plus a sprig to garnish
4 teaspoons good-quality
   drinking chocolate
   granules
1 square mint chocolate

Mint

We use organic peppermint oil in our mint chocolate bar. To add extra complexity and a really fresh flavor, the milk is first infused with mint leaves.

Simply put all the ingredients in a small saucepan and heat gently, stirring or whisking constantly to blend the ingredients. Remove from the heat just before it comes to a boil. Pour through a sieve into your favorite mug and garnish with a sprig of fresh mint.

¾ cup milk
3 teaspoon good-quality
   drinking chocolate
   granules
¾oz dark chocolate with
   ginger, finely grated,
   plus extra for garnish
Pinch of ground ginger
Pinch of ground
   cinnamon
Freshly grated nutmeg

Ginger

Rather than just stick to ginger, I've added some of the spices traditionally used in gingerbread to add a twist. Be careful when adding the spices: it's best to start with a tiny amount and then adjust later. There should be roughly equal amounts of ginger and cinnamon and just a few gratings of nutmeg. Try using the handle end of a teaspoon to administer the ginger and cinnamon. A Microplane grater is invaluable for finely grating the chocolate, and, in fact, all your grating needs.

Put all the ingredients in a small saucepan and heat gently, stirring or whisking constantly to blend the ingredients. Remove from the heat just before it comes to a boil. Taste and adjust the spices if necessary. Pour into your favorite mug and grate some extra chocolate on top before serving.

¾ cup milk
3 teaspoons good-quality
   drinking chocolate
   granules
¾oz milk chocolate, broken
   into small pieces
½ teaspoon dark molasses
1 tablespoon dark rum
Small piece (about 2in)
   of orange rind without
   pith (optional)

Milk, Rum, and Chocolate Toddy

This recipe is inspired by an old favorite ice-cream flavor: rum and raisin. Since it is difficult to incorporate raisins into a drink, I've added a little dark molasses to replicate the brown fruit notes.

Put the milk, chocolate granules, chocolate pieces, and molasses in a small saucepan and heat gently, stirring or whisking constantly to blend the ingredients. Remove from the heat just before it comes to a boil and add the rum. Pour into your favorite mug and slip in a piece of orange rind for sophistication.

¾ cup milk

3 teaspoons good-quality
drinking chocolate granules

¾oz Maya Gold chocolate

Small piece (approx 2in) of
orange rind without pith

1 vanilla bean, split and
scraped of the seeds

Small stick (approx 2in)
of cinnamon

Freshly grated nutmeg

Maya Gold

By using orange rind, a vanilla bean, a cinnamon stick, and freshly grated nutmeg in this recipe, the flavors in Maya Gold chocolate are accentuated.

Put all the ingredients (don't forget to include the vanilla bean as well as the seeds) except the nutmeg in a small saucepan and heat gently, stirring or whisking constantly to blend the ingredients and to allow the cinnamon, vanilla, and orange to infuse. Remove from the heat just before it comes to a boil. Remove the stick, bean, and peel if you'd like. Pour into your favorite mug and grate some nutmeg on top before serving.

¾ cup milk

3 teaspoons good-quality
drinking chocolate granules

1½oz almond chocolate,
finely grated, plus extra for
sprinkling

Almond

Almond is a relatively subtle flavor. Almond flavoring tends to be made with bitter almonds and has a very different flavor reminiscent of marzipan. The only way to replicate the flavor of roasted almonds in our bar is to grate the bar finely and add directly to the drink. A Microplane grater is again essential to be able to grate the almond chocolate.

Simply put all the ingredients in a small saucepan and heat gently, stirring or whisking constantly to blend the ingredients. Remove from the heat just before it comes to a boil. Pour into your favorite mug and grate some extra chocolate on top before serving.

CHURROS AND CHOCOLATE A LA ESPAÑOLA

Serves 4 to 6

1 cup water
Pinch of salt
2 cups all-purpose flour
Sunflower oil, for deep frying

For the chocolate a la Española
¾ cup milk
¼ cup plus 1 tablespoon
  heavy cream
7oz dark (70% cocoa solids)
  chocolate, chopped

Omar Allibhoy, protégé of El Bulli's Ferran Adria, offered us this recipe for *churros con chocolate*, which comes from a proper *churreria* in his beloved Madrid: "It's the version I always cook for breakfast since I was taught by the churros master at the age of 8. It's an unparalleled recipe. Eat with *chocolate a la Española*... of course."

Put the water and salt in a large saucepan and bring to a boil. Gradually add in the flour and work with a wooden spoon for 5 minutes until you have a smooth and well-mixed dough with the texture of playdough.

Fill a piping bag with the dough. It is very important that the nozzle of the bag is a 5 or 6 point star; if not, the dough will not thoroughly cook in the middle once it is deep fried. Squeeze out the dough, and, as you squeeze, grab the beginning of the churro with the tip of your thumb and draw it up toward the mouth of the piping bag while you squeeze to cut the other end of the churro with the tip of your index finger. The idea is to make a horseshoe shape that's joined at the ends. The dough is quite difficult to pipe out, but the effort is worth it!

Heat the oil to 350°F and deep-fry the churros, in batches, for a total of 2 minutes: 1 minute and 15 seconds on one side and 45 seconds on the other side. Drain the churros on paper towels to remove any excess oil and serve hot, dipped in delicious dense hot *chocolate a la Española*.

For the *chocolate a la Española*, put the milk and heavy cream in a saucepan and heat to just below boiling point. Reduce the heat to its lowest setting and add the chopped chocolate, stirring constantly until it has completely dissolved.

Tip
~ For extra depth of flavor, add some finely grated orange zest... it's superb.

STRAWBERRY PÂTE DE FRUIT

Makes about 30 pieces

1¼ cups strawberries
⅛oz powdered pectin and
  1 tablespoon superfine sugar
¾ cup superfine sugar
1½ tablespoons corn syrup
Juice of ½ small lemon
  (or more to taste)
3½oz dark (70% cocoa solids)
  chocolate, broken
  into pieces

True story: when Sharon Osbourne and Green & Black's co-founder Jo Fairley were waiting in line to meet the Queen at Buckingham Palace, Sharon swooped upon the words "Green & Black's" on Jo's name badge, and promptly confessed to having got out of bed at 2am that day to raid the fridge for a tub of our chocolate ice cream. (One of the amazing things for any of us linked with Green & Black's is the way many people we encounter instantly volunteer their favorite chocolate flavor or ice cream in our range, without us having to say a word.) So: as fans of hers, too, we're thrilled to be able to share Sharon's recipe with you.

Purée the strawberries and measure out 4½oz strawberry purée (this may vary a bit).

Mix the pectin with the 1 tablespoon of superfine sugar.

Put the strawberry purée in a small saucepan and bring to a gentle boil. Add the mixed sugar and pectin and whisk. When the purée comes back to a boil, add the ¾ cup sugar. Whisk to ensure all the sugar is incorporated and let it come to a boil once more.

Add the corn syrup and cook the mixture over medium heat until it reaches 220°F on a sugar thermometer: this should take about 3 minutes. Make sure you stir right into the edges of the pan so that the sugar doesn't burn.

When you have reached the desired temperature, remove from the heat, add the lemon juice, and pour into a mold of your choice. Leave to set for 2 hours at room temperature.

Melt the chocolate in a microwave or heatproof bowl over a pan of barely simmering water, making sure the bowl doesn't touch the water, then set aside to cool.

Dip or coat the fruit paste shapes into the chocolate and place on a marble board or a cutting board lined with silicone paper. Allow the chocolate to set before serving.

Tips

~ Pour your syrup into a small flat-bottomed plastic container and once set, you can unmold the fruit paste and cut it into various shapes: strips, diamonds, triangles, etc. Little pastry cutters are also good for cutting out the shapes. Catering and cooking equipment shops often carry little fancy shaped chocolate molds which would work equally well.

~ Try using different fruit such as passion fruit, mangoes, various melons, or citrus fruits. You will need to adjust the amount of lemon juice according to the fruit you use to get the right balance of sweetness and acidity.

CHOCOLATE MARSH-MALLOWS

Makes quite a few...

For the ganache
2½oz dark (70% cocoa
    solids) chocolate
¼ cup heavy cream
1 to 2 tablespoons hot
    water (if necessary)

For the marshmallow
3 tablespoons confectioners'
    sugar
3 tablespoons cornstarch
Vegetable oil, for greasing
1oz powdered gelatin
½ cup boiling water
2½ cups granulated sugar
¾ cup water
2 extra-large free-range
    egg whites
1 teaspoon vanilla
    extract

I love the texture of marshmallows but the (allegedly) grown-up me finds them rather sweet. I've solved the problem by swirling a simple chocolate ganache in between two layers of marshmallow before it has set.

Begin by making the ganache. Finely chop the chocolate and put in a bowl. Heat the cream, and when it comes to a boil, pour in the chocolate. Whisk until all the chocolate is melted and the mixture is smooth. If it splits and looks oily, add a tablespoon or two of hot water to bring the emulsion together. Set aside.

Sift together the confectioners' sugar and cornstarch. Oil a shallow 8 x 12in baking sheet, then dust it with some of the confectioners' sugar mix.

Combine the gelatin and the boiling water in a bowl and stir to dissolve. Set aside.

Gently heat the sugar and water in a saucepan, stirring until the sugar is dissolved. Increase the heat and, using a sugar thermometer, boil until the syrup reaches about 225°F. At this point beat the egg whites in an electric stand mixer or with a hand-held mixer until stiff. Remove the syrup from the heat when the sugar thermometer reads 250°F. Pour the dissolved gelatin into the syrup and stir to blend. Turn the mixer to its lowest setting and beat the whites while pouring the syrup in a thin stream. Once all the syrup is incorporated, add the vanilla extract to the mixture and continue to beat until thick and bulky but still pourable. If you lift up the beaters, a ribbon of marshmallow should remain on the surface for a few seconds.

Pour half the marshmallow into the prepared sheet. Drizzle the ganache over the marshmallow (warm it again slightly if it has begun to set) and use the tip of a knife to swirl the two together. Pour in the remaining marshmallow and level smooth with the back of a wet spoon or offset spatula. Put in the fridge for a good hour.

Dust your work surface with more confectioners' sugar mix. Loosen the marshmallow around the sides and bottom of the pan with an oiled offset spatula and/or your fingertips and turn it out onto the dusted surface. Cut into squares, oiling and dusting the knife between cuts, and roll them in the confectioners' sugar mix so that all surfaces are dusted. Pack into an airtight container and store in the fridge.

CHOCOLATE SEED BOMBS

Makes about 20

½ cup oats
⅓ cup sunflower seeds
1 tablespoon pumpkin seeds
7oz milk chocolate
2 tablespoons corn syrup
1 cup rice cereal

For the coating
2oz dark (70% cocoa solids)
    chocolate
⅓ cup poppy seeds

Submitted by Richard Reynolds, founder of guerrillagardening.org, this recipe is inspired by guerrilla gardening "seed bombs," which are little projectiles of seeds, compost, and clay that are used to beautify neglected patches of land. To nourish the guerrilla gardener, here's the tasty alternative in which the compost and clay have been replaced by a concoction of chocolate and syrup and the seeds are cooked for flavor rather than for flowering.

Line a large baking sheet with parchment paper.

Heat a dry frying pan over high heat and toast the oats until they begin to change color and smell a little, then transfer into a mixing bowl. Use the hot pan to toast the sunflowers seeds, followed by the pumpkin seeds, each time until they smell gently roasted and start to look shiny—be careful not to burn them. Transfer the seeds into the bowl with the oats.

Meanwhile, melt the milk chocolate in a heatproof bowl over a pan of barely simmering water, making sure the bowl doesn't touch the water, then set aside to cool. Once it has melted, add the corn syrup and stir gently.

Combine the rice cereal with the toasted oats and seeds in the mixing bowl. Pour in the melted chocolate and syrup mixture and fold in well.

Take chunks out of the mixture and roll into chestnut-size balls. Lay them on the baking sheet.

Melt the chocolate for the coating in your bowl following the method above.

Take each ball and dip half into the melted chocolate then place back on your baking sheet, chocolate side up. Once you have coated all your balls, sprinkle the chocolate tops with poppy seeds and leave to set.

You now have chocolate seed bombs to enjoy, or drop and plant, whenever you like.

Tip
~ Instead of using plain dark chocolate in the coating, we've tried butterscotch and ginger chocolate too, and they both tasted great!

CHOCOLATE FRITTERS

Makes about 24

¼ cup plus 1 tablespoon
   whole milk
¼ cup plus 2 tablespoons
   water
4 tablespoons unsalted butter
2 tablespoons superfine
   sugar, plus extra for rolling
¼ cup good-quality
   cocoa powder
½ cup all-purpose flour
2oz dark (70% cocoa solids)
   chocolate
2 extra-large free-range eggs

½ teaspoon baking soda
Sunflower oil, for deep
   frying

This recipe was given to me by Sam Hutchins, chef at Great Queen Street, a favorite restaurant of mine in London. This recipe makes for a tasty informal dessert. Fry up a batch of these fritters at the end of a meal until they are crisp on the outside but still soft within, set them in the middle of the table, and allow your friends to enjoy them at their own pace, maybe with a delicious glass of Maury (a sweet red *vins du naturels*—the ultimate wine to pair with chocolate).

Put the milk, water, butter, sugar, and cocoa powder in a saucepan and bring to a boil.

Stir the flour and baking soda into the milk mixture with a wooden spoon. Cook over low heat for 10 minutes. Remove the pan from the heat and leave the mixture to cool for 20 minutes.

Meanwhile, melt the chocolate in a heatproof bowl over a pan of barely simmering water, making sure the bowl doesn't touch the water, then set aside to cool.

Once the milk mixture is cool, beat in the eggs, one at a time, then fold in the cooled melted chocolate.

Heat a deep-fryer to 325°F or fill a heavy-bottomed saucepan with about 1 quart of sunflower oil (or any other unscented oil) and heat until a cube of bread browns in 30 seconds. The pan should be no more than a third full but with sufficient depth of oil to completely immerse the fritters. Using two tablespoons, shape the dough into fritters, and carefully lower them into the hot oil in batches of five to six. Cook for about 5 minutes. The fritters are done when they have a darkened crispy coating— they should be cooked through but still be moist inside.

Remove the fritters using a slotted spoon and lay them on a plate covered in paper towels to soak up the excess oil. You will need to change this paper a few times as it will get quite oily. Add the superfine sugar to a shallow bowl and roll the fritters to coat them in sugar. Continue these steps until all the fritters are made and serve them hot.

Tip

~ If using a frying pan, a cooking thermometer is very useful as the temperature of heated oil is hard
   to gauge by sight and can seriously affect the end result as well as being dangerous. Bring the oil up to
   temperature gradually, over low heat. Once you have reached the desired temperature, you may
   need to turn the heat off for a few minutes, then back on when the temperature drops too low and so on.

PISTACHIO AND FIG CHOCOLATE BISCOTTI

Makes 30

1⅔ cup all-purpose flour
½ cup good-quality
   cocoa powder
1½ teaspoons baking
   powder
Pinch of salt
¾ cup superfine sugar
¾ cup whole pistachios
¾ cup dried figs,
   coarsely chopped
2 extra-large free-range eggs

A *biscotto*, a hard Italian biscuit, ideally served at the end of a meal to dip into a sweet wine, is actually one of the few biscuits that does what it says on the label: it's actually baked twice (*bis* = twice, *cotto* = cooked). This one is made with two ingredients often used in Italian *dolci*: fragrant pistachios and unctuous dried figs. The added cocoa gives them a striking appearance and also makes them complement the wonderful sweet red wine of Italy, *recioto di Valpolicella*.

Preheat the oven to 375°F. Line a baking sheet with parchment paper.

Combine the flour, cocoa powder, baking powder, and salt. Add the sugar, pistachios, and dried figs and mix. Gradually add the eggs to the mixture and combine to make a dough.

Divide the dough into thirds and form into sausage shapes about 8 x 1½in. Place on the lined baking sheet and bake for 20 minutes.

Wait until just cool enough to handle and gently cut the loaves on the angle into ½in slices (try using a serrated bread knife for this) and return to the baking sheet (fit as many as you can onto the baking sheet, but you may need to do this in batches). Bake the biscotti for another 3 minutes on each side.

Enjoy, dipped in coffee.

CHOCOLATE ORANGE GINGER BISCOTTI

Makes 30

1 cup whole blanched
   almonds
2 cups bread flour
1 teaspoon baking
   powder
¾ cup superfine sugar
2oz crystallized ginger,
   finely chopped
2 extra-large free-range eggs,
   lightly beaten
1½ teaspoons orange
   extract
Confectioners' sugar, for
   dusting
5½oz dark chocolate
   with ginger

This was the winner of the recipes sent in by the publisher, Kyle Cathie Limited, in London. Emma Marijewycz, in Publicity, was inspired by her Italian grandmother's delicious biscotti and then tweaked the flavors a little to create this chocolate orange wonder.

Preheat the oven to 350°F and line one or two baking sheets with parchment paper.

Mix the flour, baking powder, and sugar in a bowl. Add the almonds, ginger, eggs, and 1 teaspoon of the orange extract. Stir to form a thick but soft dough. Dust confectioners' sugar over a clean surface, divide the mixture into three portions, and roll each one into a sausage shape.

Place the rolls on the lined sheet and flatten slightly. Bake for 20 minutes until golden brown.

Remove from the oven and carefully cut each roll on an angle into ½in-wide strips. Spread the strips in a single layer on the baking sheet and then return to the oven for 2 to 3 minutes. Remove and leave to cool.

When the biscotti have cooled, melt the chocolate in a microwave or heatproof bowl over a pan of barely simmering water, making sure the bowl doesn't touch the water. Stir in the remaining ½ teaspoon of orange extract.

Dip the cookies into the chocolate to coat half, and leave them to set on a wire rack.

VANILLA CREAM TRUFFLES

Makes about 40

½ cup heavy whipping cream
Pinch of salt
1 vanilla bean, split
  lengthwise
⅓ cup granulated sugar
9 tablespoons butter,
  at room temperature
1 to 2 tablespoons
  Mirabelle or other
  liqueur, to taste
  (optional)
About 9oz dark (70%
  cocoa solids) chocolate,
  for dipping
Good-quality cocoa powder,
  for dusting

We were first introduced to Hannah from "My Chocolate" after our co-founder Jo Fairley attended one of her fantastic workshops. We had to go and visit for ourselves, and this was one of the most delicious recipes. A great fun experience—and she is now using Green & Black's chocolate!

Put the whipping cream, salt, and vanilla bean in a saucepan over low heat and bring to just below boiling point, then reduce the heat to its lowest setting and gently simmer for about 20 minutes to allow the cream to absorb the flavor of the vanilla. Do not boil.

Remove from the heat, stir in the sugar, and allow to cool until it reaches a temperature of 68°F (room temperature).

Whisk the butter in a bowl using an electric stand mixer or hand-held mixer until it forms a soft, smooth mass. Gradually add the cream mixture, beating continuously. Add some liqueur, if using, at this stage.

If the mixture curdles (a sign that it is too cold), reheat over a pan of barely simmering water until it re-emulsifies. If it is too soft, set the bowl over iced water and beat.

Line one or two baking sheets with parchment paper. Fill a piping bag fitted with a small tip with the truffle mixture and pipe little rounds about the size of a nutmeg onto the parchment; this amount will make around 50 truffles. Transfer the sheet(s) to the freezer. After about 45 minutes, remove.

Meanwhile, melt the chocolate over a pan of barely simmering water, making sure the bowl doesn't touch the water, then set aside to cool until it reaches 105°F. Put the cocoa powder in a shallow bowl or on a plate and have a sieve on hand.

Dip the truffle fillings into the melted chocolate, then lay them in the cocoa powder. When they have set, transfer a few at a time to the sieve and shake off excess cocoa powder. Store the truffles in a freezerproof container in the fridge or, to keep them fresh for longer, in the freezer.

SIMON HOPKINSON'S CHOCOLATE PITHIVIERS

Serves 4 to 6

For the puff pastry
1¾ cups all-purpose flour,
    plus extra for dusting
Pinch of salt
8oz (2 sticks) cold unsalted
    butter, cut into small pieces
Juice of ½ lemon
½ cup iced water
1 extra-large free-range egg,
    beaten, for glazing
Confectioners' sugar,
    for dusting

For the crème pâtissière
¾ cup whole milk
1 vanilla bean, split lengthwise
3 extra-large free-range
    egg yolks

⅓ cup superfine sugar
3 tablespoons all-purpose flour

**For the chocolate
    mixture**
8 tablespoons (1 stick)
    unsalted butter, softened
½ cup superfine sugar
2 extra-large free-range eggs
⅔ cup ground almonds
⅓ cup good-quality cocoa
    powder
½ tablespoon dark rum
3½oz dark (70% cocoa solids)
    chocolate, chopped into
    small chocolate-chip
    sized pieces

Whipped cream, to serve

While partaking in a luncheon at Rowley Leigh's consistently good Café Anglais (if you find yourself in London, go there and order the Parmesan custard with anchovy toasts; then order it again), I spotted Simon Hopkinson at the bar. Being one of my food writing heroes (if you don't have any of his books, buy them—all of them) and with the best part of a bottle of wine in me to give me the required courage, I walked up to him and asked if he would contribute a recipe to the book. Slightly and understandably taken aback for a few seconds, he was then charm itself and offered me this recipe from *Roast Chicken and Other Stories*, a chocolate pithivier, which is, in layman's terms, a very tasty chocolate and almond puff pastry.

First make the pastry, preferably the day before or at least several hours in advance.

Sift the flour and salt together into a bowl and add the butter.

Loosely mix, but don't rub the two together in the normal way of pastry-making. The idea is to handle the butter as little as possible while still incorporating it into the flour. A good way of doing this is to use two butter knives and cut the butter pieces in a cross action.

Mix the lemon juice with the iced water and pour into the butter/flour mixture. Using a metal spoon, gently mix together until it forms a cohesive mass.

Turn on to a cool surface and shape into a thick rectangle. Flour the work surface and gently roll the pastry into a rectangle measuring about 7 x 4in.

Fold one third of the rectangle over toward the center and fold the remaining third over that. Lightly press together and rest the pastry in the fridge for 10 minutes.

Return the pastry to the same position on the work surface and turn it through 90 degrees. Roll it out to the same dimensions as before, and fold and rest again in the same way.

Repeat this turning, rolling, folding, and resting process three more times. (Phew! This is the moment when you wish you'd bought ready-made pastry!) Wrap the pastry in plastic wrap and leave in the fridge for several hours or overnight.

To make the crème pâtissière, put the milk and vanilla bean in a saucepan over low heat and bring gently to a boil.

Whisk together the egg yolks, sugar, and flour until light and fluffy. Gradually pour the hot milk on to the egg mixture whisking lightly. Return the mixture to the saucepan and cook gently until it thickens. Do not let it come to a boil. Pour through a sieve into a bowl, discard the vanilla bean, and chill.

To make the chocolate mixture, cream the butter and sugar until light and fluffy. Add the eggs and beat again. Add the ground almonds and cocoa powder and beat again. Add the rum with the cooled crème pâtissière and finally fold in the chopped chocolate. Chill.

Preheat the oven to 400°F and grease a baking sheet.

Roll out the pastry to a thickness of about ⅛in. Cut it into four 4in squares and four 6in squares. Place the smaller squares on a floured board.

Using an ice-cream scoop or tablespoon, place a scoop of the chocolate mixture in the center of each small square of pastry. Brush the pastry edges with some of the beaten egg, place the larger squares of pastry on top, and press down and around firmly to seal, ensuring there are no air bubbles.

Use a 4in round pastry cutter to cut the filled pastry squares into neat rounds. Press and seal together the edges with a fork to form a decorative pattern. Brush the pithiviers with the remaining beaten egg and dust lightly with confectioners' sugar.

Place on the baking sheet and cook in the oven for 15 to 20 minutes or until the pastry is well risen, shiny, and golden brown. Remove from the oven, dust lightly with some more confectioners' sugar, and serve hot with whipped cream.

Tips

~ *When making the pastry, keep note of how many turns you have made since it is easy to lose track. You may also notice that bits of butter are still visible at the end of the last turn—this is fine, as it is those little lumps of butter that, on melting, release steam between the pastry layers, causing it to rise.*

~ *This recipe gives enough pastry to make four pithiviers in the first batch. There is also the option to make another two from the trimmings. These won't always rise as well as the first ones, but only marginally so. If you want to make these extra pithiviers, gather the trimmings, gently press them together, and roll them out as described above.*

~ *For a richer, more golden finish, separate the egg and use the yolk as the glaze. You can use the egg white as the "glue."*

TOM AIKENS' CHOCOLATE CRÊPES

Makes 18 to 20

4 tablespoons (½ stick)
  unsalted butter, melted
2oz dark (70%cocoa solids)
  chocolate, broken
  into pieces
¼ cup superfine sugar, plus
  extra for sprinkling
1¾ cups all-purpose flour
¼ cup good-quality
  cocoa powder
4 large free-range eggs plus
  2 egg yolks, beaten
2 cups 1% milk
Oil for cooking

Tom Aikens of Tom Aikens Restaurant in London developed this recipe based on a recipe he used to make with his mother. Cocoa was added to make the crêpes delicious and chocolatey—they remain an all-time favorite of his.

Gently melt together the butter and chocolate over low heat. Set aside.

Mix together the sugar, flour, and cocoa powder and then sift into a large bowl. Make a well in the middle and then add the beaten eggs then the milk, then the melted butter and chocolate.

Pass the batter through a fine sieve and leave to rest for a couple of hours.

When you are ready to cook, heat up a large non-stick frying pan and rub with a little oil. Add enough crêpe mix to the pan, tilting it from side to side, to make a thin cover.

Cook for a minute on each side and slide the crêpe out on to a warm plate lined with parchment paper and sprinkle with superfine sugar. Continue to cook the crêpes until all the batter is used, layering each one with a sprinkling of sugar as you go.

Serve immediately, perhaps with some chocolate sauce or mousse.

Tips

~ *To give an even coating of oil on your frying pan, use a paper towel to spread it over the hot pan.*

~ *To prevent burning, keep your pan well oiled and cook the crêpes over medium heat.*

~ *If you think the mixture is too thick, add a little extra milk.*

THYME AND CHOCOLATE TRUFFLES

½ cup heavy whipping cream
½oz thyme sprigs
7oz dark (70% cocoa
   solids) chocolate,
   broken into pieces
Good-quality cocoa,
   for dusting

Makes about 20

Jo Wood became interested in organic food more than two decades ago, long before it became commonplace on every supermarket shelf. Back then it would have been impossible to make her recipe below with organic ingredients, even with the relatively few needed here, whereas now it's easy. Jo has used thyme to infuse her cream before making the ganache, which works beautifully. Try replacing the thyme with other herbs such as rosemary, mint or basil, experimenting with infusion amounts and times for the flavour that suits your palate best.

Cover a large, heavy cutting board or a baking sheet tightly and completely with plastic wrap or parchment paper.

In a small saucepan, bring the cream and thyme to a simmer over low heat. Remove from the heat and allow to infuse for 10 minutes. Strain and return the cream to the heat until it reaches a simmer again. Taste, and don't be afraid to use your own judgement: if you think the thyme flavor isn't strong enough, leave the herb in the hot cream for another 5 minutes or so.

Place the chocolate in a large mixing bowl and immediately pour the cream over it. Mix thoroughly until all the chocolate has melted.

Allow the mixture to cool at room temperature until it is set, this will take about 1½ hours.

Once the mixture has set, use a teaspoon to spoon out bite-sized pieces. Dust your palms lightly with cocoa powder to keep them from sticking and roll the pieces into balls using your hands.

Immediately roll the truffles in sifted cocoa powder and place on the prepared board to set completely.

L'ARTISAN'S CHOCOLATE MARTINI

Chocolate olives
⅓ cup whole almonds
2oz dark chocolate
1oz white chocolate
Green food coloring
(a few drops)

Per cocktail
3 tablespoons vodka
1½ tablespoons Lillet
or vermouth

Gerard and Anne, good friends of mine who run *L'Artisan du Chocolat*, contributed one of my favorite recipes in our first book; their chocolate and salted caramel tart. For this book they've let me have a couple of chocolate cocktail recipes that they serve in their Notting Hill store. Both take a bit of preparation (the chocolate vodka for the chocolate martini takes at least a week to make but once it's infused you have enough for fifteen cocktails) but are worth the effort.

Rather than using sweet chocolate liquor, we recommend infusing vodka for as long as possible with cocoa nibs—100% chocolate or the darkest chocolate possible. Add 1oz of cacao per 1 (750ml) bottle of vodka; let it infuse for a minimum of 1 week, shaking it regularly. The vodka will turn a gold amber color and take on a taste of bitter chocolate.

Roast the almonds and let them cool. Melt the chocolate over a pan of barely simmering water, making sure the bowl doesn't touch the water. Melt the white chocolate in the same way and add the green food coloring. Keep the melted chocolate warm.

Place the cool almonds in a bowl and drizzle with a little bit of warm dark chocolate (too much and the nuts will stick). Mix furiously in circles with a spoon until the chocolate sets (without getting the almonds to stick together). You need to work in a cool place for this. Repeat until all the dark chocolate is used (if you are building up too much chocolate in the bowl, it means that you are adding the chocolate too fast). Do the same with the green chocolate to build a green layer.

Roll in your warm hands to give a little shine. Set aside for a few hours for the chocolate to crystallize (if you can stop eating them).

Chill the martini glass. Fill a cocktail shaker with ice. Add a chocolate olive to the bottom or side of the glass.

Pour the vodka in the shaker. Add the Lillet or vermouth. Stir with a cocktail spoon (don't shake).

Double strain and serve very cold

Tips

~If you cannot get hold of cocoa nibs then use 1oz of 70% dark chocolate, finely chopped or grated, and 1 tablespoon of cocoa powder per bottle of vodka. After a week or so, strain through a coffee filter and it's ready to use.
~For a drier martini, reduce the amount of vermouth to taste (2 teaspoons works pretty well).
~Roast the almonds at 350°C for approximately 8 minutes or until you can smell them. They should be colored within but not burnt.

MATCHA (GREEN TEA) WHITE CHOCOLATE NEW ORLEANS FIZZ

Matcha drinking chocolate (enough for 4 cocktails)
½ cup whole milk
1½ tablespoons light cream
1¾oz Artisan matcha bar or 1½oz good quality white chocolate and ¼oz of fine matcha tea powder (the better the tea, the better the drink)

Per cocktail
1½ tablespoons gin
1½ tablespoons lemon juice
1 cocktail spoon superfine sugar
3 tablespoons matcha cold drink
1 extra-large free-range egg white
Sparkling water or soda, to top up

Also called the New Orleans Fizz, this drink was created in 1888 by Henry Ramos. All you need to make it are several common bar ingredients and strength. The Ramos Fizz needs to be shaken like mad (5 minutes of furious shaking) to emulsify the cream, egg, and spirit and produce a properly frothy drink. Indeed, Ramos himself employed a brigade of bartenders who passed the shaker from one to the next until the drink reached the desired consistency. The original was made with cream and orange water so here is L'Artisan's version with creamy white chocolate and matcha.

Make the matcha drinking chocolate a few hours in advance. Heat the milk and cream until very hot but not burning.

Break the chocolate in small pieces or shavings. Pour the hot mix onto the chocolate and matcha and emulsify with a spoon/spatula. Leave to cool.

When completely cold, sieve (and liquidize if required) and move on to making the cocktail.

Put the gin, lemon juice, and superfine sugar in a cocktail shaker. Add the matcha drinking chocolate (if very frothy, add a little over). Take the egg white and shake it to break it. Add 1 cocktail spoon of egg white. Add lots of ice.

Shake for 4 minutes minimum (when made originally the New Orleans Fizz was shaken for 10 minutes and passed along a long lines of cocktail makers). Prepare a collins glass with ice to top. Double sieve into the glass.

Top up with sparkling water or soda water.

Tips
~ *You can buy matcha tea from Japanese food stores but if you can't find it, substitute with the best green tea you can find, ground as finely as possible using a spice mill or a mortar and pestle.*

205

INDEX